CHOCOLATE
THE BRITISH CHOCOLATE INDUSTRY

Paul Chrystal
and Joe Dickinson
with photographs by Mark Sunderland

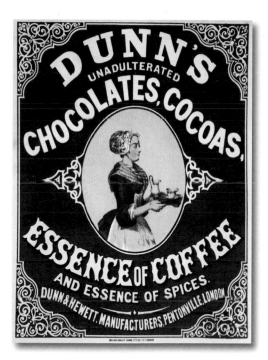

SHIRE PUBLICATIONS

Published in Great Britain in 2014 by Shire Publications Ltd,
PO Box 883, Oxford OX1 9PL, United Kingdom.
PO Box 3985, New York, NY 10185-3983, USA.
E-mail: shire@shirebooks.co.uk   www.shirebooks.co.uk

A CIP catalogue record for this book is available from the
British Library.

Shire Library no. 497.   ISBN-13: 978 0 74780 841 1

Paul Chrystal and Joe Dickinson have asserted their rights
under the Copyright, Designs and Patents Act, 1988, to
be identified as the authors of this book.

Designed by Tony Truscott Designs, Sussex, UK
and typeset in Perpetua and Gill Sans.
Printed in China through World Print Ltd.

14 15 16 17 18   11 10 9 8 7 6 5 4 3 2

COVER IMAGE
A selection of Cadbury chocolate products. (Courtesy
of Mike Ashworth.)

TITLE PAGE IMAGE
A showcard from around 1890. Dunn's was a major force
in late Victorian coffee and chocolate manufacturing, with
frequent support from the *British Medical Journal* regarding
medical benefits.

CONTENTS PAGE IMAGE
A typical scene from a chocolate house capturing the
general hubbub and fashionable socialising that went on.
It is taken from a mural adorning the walls of a dining
room at Cadbury's in the 1940s.

DEDICATION
Everybody wants a box of chocolates and a long stem rose.

Leonard Cohen

ACKNOWLEDGEMENTS
Thanks go to the following for their help and support in
my research and in the provision of images used in this
book; without them it would be much diminished: Melvyn
Browne; Dudley Chignall, CocoCubs; Rachael Chrystal for
reading the final draft; Robert Cunningham-Brown, Caley
of Norwich Ltd; Sarah Foden, Cadbury UK; Joe Dickinson
for photographs of his Rowntree's collection; Frenchay
Village Museum, Bristol; Beth Hurrell, Joseph Rowntree
Foundation; Alex Hutchinson, Nestlé Heritage, York;
Dr Amanda Jones and colleagues, Borthwick Institute,
University of York; Fergus Loudon, Thomas Tunnock Ltd;
Sarah McKee, Bettys & Taylors of Harrogate; Norfolk
Record Office. Also to Anne, Rachael, Michael and
Rebecca Chrystal for sourcing and procuring the research
materials ... and then promptly eating them.

Shire Publications is supporting the Woodland Trust, the UK's leading woodland conservation charity, by funding the dedication of trees.

CONTENTS

Rhvmvilig im Einnehme   Fruchtbar im Cutfuchen.

Der Chocolat.

EARLY DAYS

CHOCOLATE GROWS ON TREES; so, therefore, does money, as Montezuma and the Aztecs proved. It grows on trees in the form of cocoa powder from the seeds or beans of the cacao tree, *Theobroma cacao* – literally, 'cocoa, food of the gods'. 'Cacao' means 'bitter juice' in Mayan. The main growing areas are central and eastern South America and West Africa, all within 20 degrees of the Equator, below 1,000 feet in the shade and at a minimum temperature of 16°C. Between thirty and forty white pulp-covered seeds are to be found in the average, football-sized pod; it fruits all year round. In the very early days the beans were sun dried and the kernels or nibs (up to half their weight is made up of fat, or cacao butter) were roasted, shelled and crushed into a paste called cacao liquor – liquor in the liquid essence sense – and then made into cakes. These were then crumbled and immersed in water to form liquid chocolate. The drink was taken both hot and cold, thickened to make a soup or re-dried to make cakes. Four hundred or so beans make 1lb of chocolate.

There is some evidence that the pre-Mayan Olmecs from 1500 BC up to about 400 BC and, later, the Izapan, knew cacao. But it was probably the Mayans who cultivated, manufactured and consumed chocolate on a large scale from around AD 600, in a bitter liquid form they called *xocolatl*. Cacao beans and roasting griddles have been found in excavated tombs bearing hieroglyphs which spell '*kakaw*'. These finds also tell us that the Mayans drank it unsweetened or sometimes spiced with vanilla, honey or chilli pepper. The Aztecs conquered the Mayans in around AD 1200 and started chocolate's association with divinity by worshipping Quetzalcoatl as the bringer of chocolate. Cacao beans had been used as symbols for numbers by the Mayans and we know that the Mayans and others had traded with cacao: to give some context, a porter's daily pay amounted to about one hundred beans, a fresh avocado cost three beans, a rabbit cost eight beans, a prostitute was negotiable around ten depending on the service required, a turkey or a slave one hundred.

But it was Montezuma II (reigned 1502–20) who really exploited the fiscal power of chocolate: he adopted cacao as currency in place of gold,

Opposite:
German nobleman
being served
chocolate by
a buxom lady
in Martin
Engelbrecht's *Der
Chocolat* (c. 1740).
Compare the
picture on page 84,
260 years later.

Above: Picking cocoa pods in what was then the Gold Coast, now Ghana.

established a bean bank and allowed tribute to be paid in cocoa beans. Ferdinand Columbus (Christopher's son) tells us, 'those almonds which in New Spain are used for money ... they seemed to hold these almonds at great price.'

Montezuma reputedly drank fifty cups of chocolate every day because he believed it to be an aphrodisiac, thus helping to establish chocolate's pseudo-medical and sexual reputation. To the Aztecs chocolate was very much a beverage for the rich and regal, typically served at the end of a meal in much the same way as port or mint chocolates are today. Like the Mayans, the Aztecs adulterated it with pimento, pepper, and the ground-down bones of the dead. Giralamo Benzoni, in his 1575 *History of the New World*, considered it 'more a drink for pigs than humanity', and José de Acosta, Jesuit missionary and naturalist, in his *Natural and Moral History* of 1590, describes it thus: '[chocolate] disgusts ... it has a foam

Right: Piles of cocoa pods destined for the Rowntree factory in Agbado, Nigeria.

on top, or a scum-like bubbling.' Such antipathy gradually evaporated as Spanish ways and culture infiltrated local habits and diet. The Spanish drank it hot rather than cold and added more familiar spices such as black pepper and cinnamon.

The conquistadores went looking for El Dorado but they found chocolate too; Hernán Cortés was unimpressed when he tasted it as a post-prandial treat with Montezuma but, unlike Columbus, he did recognise its commercial potential, for example as pay for porters. He promptly took the recipe and methods of cultivation and production back to Spain and Charles V.

Charles's people added cane sugar to make it sweet and invented the *molinillo* to froth it up; the king was impressed to hear from Cortés that chocolate was an energy drink – allowing a man to march all day without need for food. For most of the sixteenth century, chocolate was largely confined to Spain, but its spread to neighbouring countries was inevitable. Visitors to the Spanish

French engraving depicting (top) an Aztec with his *chocolatièr* and cup; the lower picture is a cocoa tree branch with vanilla beans, which would have been used for flavouring.

Cortés meets Montezuma and paves the way for the introduction of cocoa to Europe.

Frontispiece of Cardinal Brancaccio's 1639 Latin reference work on cocoa showing Neptune, Roman god of the sea, receiving a gift of chocolate from America personified – symbolising the arrival of chocolate in Europe.

court in the seventeenth century carried the recipe back to their various homes: the explorer Antonio Carletti detailed the process of cacao cultivation for the Italian court; and Anne of Austria, daughter of Philip III, took it back to France when she married Louis XIII in 1615 – along with a maid exclusively dedicated to chocolate preparation and nicknamed La Molina.

Philip II's physician, Francisco Hernandez, had as early as 1577 connected the medical and aphrodisiac properties of chocolate when he confirmed that it not only 'alleviated intestinal pains and colic' but also 'excited the venereal appetite'. To Dr Giovanni Batiste Felici, though, writing in 1728, chocolate was one of the 'many disorders which Mankind has introduced to shorten their lives', changing normally quiet people into angry chatterboxes and turning children hyperactive. Geronimo Piperni's eulogy is more typical, describing chocolate as a 'divine, celestial drink, the sweat of the stars, the vital seed … universal medicine'.

If you were to believe the socialite and gossip the Marquise de Sévigné, chocolate had a defining role in embryology: one of her missives in 1671 tells us that 'The Marquise de Coëtlogon took so much chocolate during her pregnancy last year that she produced a small boy as black as the devil, who died.' She probably epitomised French society generally, blowing hot and cold over chocolate: one day in 1671 she saw it as an ideal soporific; two months later 'it is cursed ... the source of vapours and palpitations ... suddenly lights a continuous fever in you that leads to death.' By October, though, it was the perfect nutritious *digestif*.

Chocolate, as we have seen, improved sexual prowess: the conquistador Bernal Diaz noted that the Aztec aristocracy took chocolate 'for success with women'. To the notorious Giacomo Casanova it was as good an icebreaker as champagne and, like Samuel Pepys, he enjoyed a morning draught to set the day off. Louis XVI's mistresses, Mesdames du Barry and de Pompadour, played their parts in sexing up chocolate, however unwittingly: du Barry was scurrilously accused of exciting her lovers with chocolate to satisfy her own lust. Pompadour, on the other hand, was reputedly frigid and, according to Stanley Loomis, used hot chocolate along with 'aphrodisiacs, truffle and celery soup to stir a sensuality that was at best sluggish.'

An early Catalonian tile panel (1720) showing busy chocolate activity: the men are serving the ladies with the chocolate, which is being prepared in the bottom right corner.

CHOCOLATE COMES TO ENGLAND

Eidentify NGLAND'S EARLY ENCOUNTERS with chocolate were far from auspicious.
Thomas Gage noted in 1579:

> When we have taken a good prize, a ship laden with cocoa, in anger and
> wrath we have hurled overboard this good commodity not regarding the
> worth and goodness of it, but calling it in bad Spanish *cagaruta de carnero*, or
> sheep shit in good English.

José de Acosta in his 1590 *Natural and Moral History* tells us that an English
corsair burnt 100,000 loads of cacao in the port of Guatulco in New Spain,
the equivalent of 2.4 billion beans. It was a Parisian shopkeeper who opened
the first chocolate shop in London, in June 1657. The 23 June 1659 edition
of Needham's *Mercurius Politicus* ran the following advertisement:

> An excellent West India drink called chocolate, in Bishopsgate Street, in
> Queen's Head Alley, at a Frenchman's house being the first man who did sell
> it in England ... ready at any time, and also unmade at reasonable rates ...
> it cures and preserves the body of many diseases.

Chocolate makes an appearance in 1658 as a 'compounded Indian drink,
whose chief ingredient is a fruit called Cacao' in Edward Phillips's *The New
World of English Words, or, A General dictionary Containing the Interpretation of such
Hard Words as are derived from other Languages*. M. Sury's Oxford chocolate
house pamphlet in 1660 describes chocolate as a panacea:

> By this pleasing drink health is preserved, sickness diverted. It cures
> consumptions and Coughs of the Lungs; it expels poison, cleanseth the teeth,
> and sweetneth the Breath; provoketh Urine; cureth the stone and strangury,
> maketh Fatt and Corpulent, faire and aimeable.

And when it comes to its benefits to infertile women he is quite poetic:

Nor need the Women longer grieve,
Who spend their oyle yet not Conceive,
For 'tis a Help Immediate,
If such but Lick of Chocolate.

James Wadsworth wittily declared in his *Curious History of the Nature and Quality of Chocolate*:

Twill make Old Women Young and Fresh,
Create New Motion of the Flesh,
And cause them Long for you know what,
If they but taste of Chocolate.

Pepys' diary entries show how it was very much part of his society, thus confirming chocolate as one of the drinks of choice among men of influence and affluence. On the morning of 24 April 1661 he used it as a hangover cure after Charles II's coronation, waking up 'with my head in a sad taking through last night's drink which I am sorry for. So rose and went out with Mr Creede to drink our morning draft, which he did give me chocolate to settle my stomach.'

In 1780, Joseph Fry was commissioned to supply the Royal Navy with a ration of chocolate in cocoa slab form to replace rum and to provide the sailors with something a little more nutritious to go with their ship's biscuit. In the 1850s Fry's tins were sent to the troops fighting in the Crimean War. In literary circles too, chocolate was beginning to make its mark. Hester Thrale Piozzi tells us how Samuel Johnson used chocolate as a replacement for alcohol: 'he took his chocolate liberally, pouring in large quantities of cream, or even melted butter.' Voltaire's Candide learns that the spread of syphilis throughout Europe by Columbus's explorers was a fair price to pay for the simultaneous introduction of chocolate and cochineal.

The works of the notorious Marquis de Sade have frequent references to chocolate, consumed before and after sex, and it features regularly in his orgies. His petulant letters from prison to Mme de Sade (Renée de Montreuil) betray a genuine personal craving; this from 16 May 1779:

The sponge cake is not at all what I asked for. 1st, I wanted it iced all over ... 2nd I wanted it to have chocolate inside as black as the devil's arse is black from smoke, and there isn't even the least trace of chocolate. I beg you to have it sent to me at the first opportunity ... the cakes must smell of it, as if you're biting into a bar of chocolate.

De Sade's greatest chocolate moment is told by Louis Petit de Bachaumont in his *Mémoires secrets pour servir à l'histoire de la République des Lettres*: at a ball given by de Sade the host laced the chocolate pastilles with Spanish fly, a well known aphrodisiac:

> It proved to be so potent that those who ate the pastilles began to burn with unchaste ardour and to carry on as if in the grip of the most amorous frenzy ... even the most respectable of women were unable to resist the uterine rage that stirred within them. And so it was that M de Sade enjoyed the favours of his sister-in-law ... several persons died of their frightful priapic excesses, and others are still quite sick.

Musically speaking, chocolate makes an appearance in Mozart's *Così fan Tutte*, premiered in 1790. The maid, Despina, bewails her lot and, overcome by temptation and the smell of chocolate, declares:

> I've been beating the chocolate for half an hour, now it is ready ... O gracious mistresses, why should you get the real thing and I only the smell of it? By Bacchus I'm going to taste it; oh, it's so good!

White's, one of London's premier chocolate houses, in St James's. White's went on to become one of London's leading gentlemen's clubs.

Chocolate houses in London were generally concentrated around Covent Garden and St James's, competing, London resident (1668–88) Lorenzo Magolotti tells us, with the ubiquitous coffee houses as somewhere good to eat, play cards and dice, gamble, converse, and to drink cider, sherbet (a drink then), tea and cock ale (beer with bits of fowl in it). Jonathan Swift was less impressed: he describes White's Chocolate House as a place to be 'fleeced and corrupted by fashionable gamblers and profligates'.

White's was opened in 1693 by the Italian Francis White and by 1709 had achieved such a fashionable reputation that Richard Steele wrote his pieces for *The Tatler* there: 'All accounts of Gallantry, Pleasure and Entertainment shall be under the article of White's Chocolate House, Poetry under that of ....' In Alexander Pope's *Dunciad* it was where you went to 'teach oaths to youngsters and to nobles wit'.

The Cocoa Tree also enjoyed Steele's patronage, this time along with Joseph Addison, who wrote articles for *The Spectator* from there when it was launched in 1711.

White's Club, on the left of St. James's Palace.
(*From a Drawing of the time of Queen Anne.*)

Left: William Hogarth (1697–1764) set the gambling scene in *The Rake's Progress* at White's, thus telling us a lot about the sorts of things that went on there – and at other chocolate houses, no doubt.

Below: Chocolate being served in an eighteenth-century chocolate house during a gambling session.

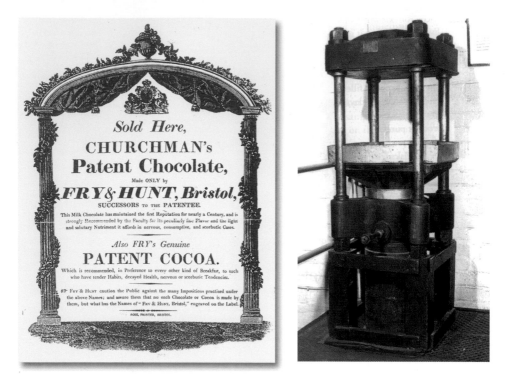

Above:
Advertisements
for Walter
Churchman's
Patent Chocolate,
describing the
patent rights
bought by Joseph
Fry and John Hunt.

Above right: Van
Houten's press.

Addison ranked chocolate alongside 'romances' and 'novels' as one of life's great 'inflamers'. Soon chocolate house owners were realising the business opportunities their establishments offered and so rewrote their business plans to convert them into havens for the rich, the privileged and the male and, in doing so, forged the origins of the English gentlemen's club.

But it was a Dutch chemist and confectioner, Coenraad van Houten, who made the real breakthrough in the development of eating chocolate; and it would be to him that both George Cadbury and Joseph Rowntree went sooner or later when developing their respective businesses. In 1828 he invented a hydraulic press which squeezed out most of the cocoa butter from the liquor, thus reducing the cocoa butter content from over 50 per cent to 27 per cent and leaving chocolate powder or, as we know it, cocoa. Then, in the 1880s, by adding alkalis such as potassium or sodium carbonate in to the liquor (a process known as 'Dutching') Van Houten was able to render it darker, mellower, more mixable and softer and, with added sugar, sweeter. This revolution led the way to the mass production of cheaper chocolate in powder and solid form.

Along with the squalid deployment of tens of thousands of slaves, mechanisation soon began to help increase production and foster commercialisation. It was Joseph Fry & Sons of Bristol who led the way when

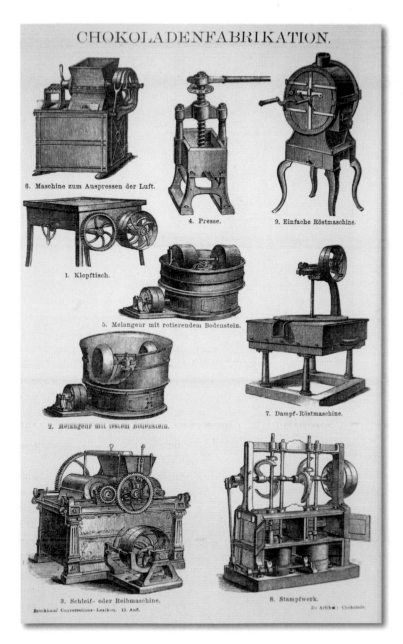

CHOKOLADENFABRIKATION.

6. Maschine zum Auspressen der Luft.

4. Presse.

9. Einfache Röstmaschine.

1. Klopftisch.

5. Melangeur mit rotierendem Bodenstein.

2. Melangeur mit festem Bodenstein.

7. Dampf-Röstmaschine.

3. Schleif- oder Reibmaschine.

8. Stampfwerk.

Brockhaus' Conversations-Lexikon. 13. Aufl.

Zu Artikel: Chokolade.

Late-nineteenth-century chocolate-making machinery as depicted in Brockhaus's *Konversations Lexikon*; the Germans were leaders in this field. The machines are: (1) shell hammering table; (2) mixer with fixed stones; (3) grinder; (4) cocoa butter extractor press; (5) mixer with rotating stones; (6) air bubble extractor; (7) steam roaster; (8) moulder; (9) roaster.

in 1761 Fry bought a watermill and warehouse and established a sales agency network in fifty-three English towns. In 1795 Joseph Fry effectively industrialised chocolate production in England when he started using a James

Watt steam engine to grind his beans. Reductions by Gladstone in the punitive duty on chocolate in 1852 from 2s to 1d per pound also had a profound effect on consumer affordability and demand.

The Temperance movement took to chocolate with gusto, establishing British Workman houses to compete with alcohol-serving public houses; they even published a guide instructing how to set up and run these establishments. The Quakers had strong links with the movement and so began the association of Quakers with chocolate. Messrs Fry, Cadbury, Terry and Rowntree made 'conversation lozenges' and dragées which carried such romantic messages as 'Do you love me?' and 'No, I won't ask Mama', but the Quakers poured sobering cold water on it all by distributing their sweets with such blunt and uncompromising messages as 'Misery, sickness and poverty are the effect of drunkenness.'

The manufacture of drinking chocolate created up to 30 per cent discarded cocoa butter. The solution to the problem of this wastage was to make it into eating chocolate, and Joseph Fry & Sons was again the pioneer. It had been making drinking chocolate since 1728 and in 1847 it developed eating chocolate in bar form by adding some of the cocoa butter back into the mix, producing a thinner paste that was easier to mould. Cadbury followed: George Cadbury visited Van Houten in Holland and brought back one of his machines, thus enabling the firm to start producing its Cocoa Essence from 1866.

Sales of chocolate in 1852 totalled 9 tons, rising to 12,000 tons in 1904. Henry Mayhew's 1851 *London Labour and the London Poor* gives us some idea of the relative size of the confectionery market at the time: £10,000 per annum compared with £31,200 for tea and coffee, £19,448 for hot eels, £14,000 for baked potatoes, £11,400 for fried fish, £6,000 for muffins and crumpets, and £3,000 for pies. There were 230 sweet-sellers in the capital. In Manchester there were two confectionery shops in 1772, rising to 308 in 1872 (by comparison there were 804 butchers and 374 bakers). Confectionery schools were established, the most famous being the Ladies' Confiserie Company and the piping and ornamentation school on Tottenham Court Road.

Switzerland then took centre stage: and the work they did leading to the production of milk

Sir Hans Sloane (of Sloane Square fame) sold his milk chocolate in Greek Street, Soho, 'prepared after his original recipe by Cadbury Brothers' between 1849 and 1875. The trade card includes medical claims and testimonials and insists that this product is the genuine article.

chocolate was felt all over Europe, including England. Philip Suchard first came across chocolate when his mother sent him to collect a supply from an apothecary in Neuchatel (at a cost of SFr 6,00 – equal to three days' pay for a workman); he set up his confectionery business in 1826. Charles-Amédée Kohler introduced hazelnuts into chocolate in 1831 in his Lausanne factory. In 1876, Rodolphe Lindt introduced conching – a process which resulted in a smoother, more pleasant flavour we now know as fondant chocolate. A conche is a container filled with metal beads, which act as grinders; before conching chocolate has a gritty texture but conching produces smoother cocoa and sugar particles which cannot be detected by the tongue. The longer the conching process the smoother the chocolate. The high point though was the development of milk chocolate in 1879 by Swiss manufacturer Daniel Peter, who combined powdered milk – which had recently been developed by Henri Nestlé as an infant food – with chocolate and cocoa butter to produce a solid that was easy to mould and shape. In 1899 Jean Tobler made the transition from confectioner to manufacturer in Bern, turning out the distinctive bar we still see today. The same year Lindt merged with Johann Rudolf Sprungli of Zurich to form Chocoladefabriken Lindt und Sprungli.

The milk chocolate bar and the chocolate-coated sweet were thus born. With the new mechanisation, the chocolate industry was totally transformed in England and in the rest of Europe. Chocolate was now being eaten as well as drunk although it would not be until the early years of the twentieth century that sales of eating chocolate outstripped drinking chocolate.

A Lehmann's
conching machine.

17

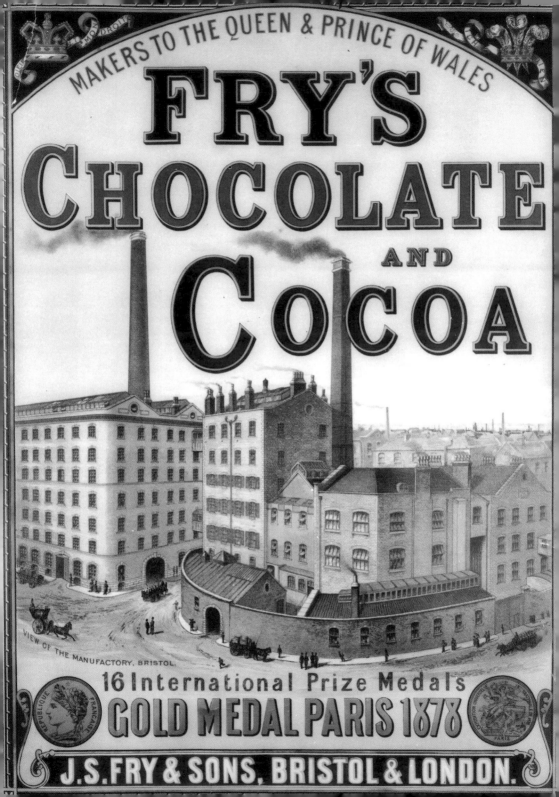

FRY'S OF BRISTOL

FRY'S was at the forefront of developments in chocolate production in England in the eighteenth and nineteenth centuries, and was appointed to the Royal Household as cocoa and chocolate manufacturer by no fewer than seven monarchs. Walter Churchman had been running what was obviously a successful chocolate shop in the city and in 1728 was granted Letters Patent from George II – a highly prestigious and attractive honour. Things accelerated in 1761 when Joseph Fry, a Quaker physician (entrepreneur, industrialist and businessman *par excellence*), with John Vaughan, bought Walter Churchman's chocolate business, which then became Fry, Vaughan & Co.

The coffee and chocolate houses in nearby fashionable Bath soon became a lucrative cocoa market. At the same time Fry's acquired patent rights and recipes for the manufacture of drinking chocolate. The company moved in 1777 from Newgate Street to upmarket Union Street to tap the wealthy clientele there; two years later, on Joseph's death, his widow, Anna Fry, took over and renamed the company Anna Fry & Son.

That son was Joseph Storrs Fry, who was in charge from 1795; it was he who industrialised and revolutionised chocolate manufacture when he introduced the Watt steam engine into the manufacturing process. On Anna's death in 1803 a Dr Hunt joined the company, thus leading to another re-badging as Fry & Hunt; on Hunt's retirement Joseph Storrs's sons (Joseph II, Francis and Richard) became partners and the company was renamed J. S. Fry & Sons – by then England's largest chocolate producer. In 1835 Fry's was using 40 per cent of the cocoa imported into Britain with sales of £12,000 per annum.

Until 1853 it was French chocolate which enjoyed the best reputation in Britain and the general belief was that anything British simply could not compete. But then Fry's produced its Cream Stick – the first chocolate confectionery to be produced on an industrial scale. Hitherto chocolate had been a luxury beyond the budgets of most people but this was a 'value-for-money bar'. The popularity of French chocolate receded to the extent that

Opposite:
A fine poster
from 1880 showing
the Fry factory in
Bristol and proudly
boasting the
awards and Royal
Appointment the
firm had won
by 1878.

19

All chocolate makers were at pains to emphasise the nutritional benefits of their products: the milkmaids and pails do the trick here.

Below left:
A showcard promoting the warming qualities of Fry's cocoa and chocolate (on the road to Bristol).

Below right:
A Fry's showcard from the 1930s.

Fry's even received a brevet appointing them manufacturers of cocoa and chocolate to the Imperial House of Napoleon III.

So, having mechanised chocolate production with steam power and having pioneered eating chocolate in 1847, Fry's could claim another first when in 1866 they started production of the direct descendant of Fry's Cream Stick, Fry's Chocolate Cream – a fondant cream-filled chocolate bar, which was remoulded in 1875 to the shape it still has today. With deeper moulds than the standard bar, the chocolate filling is tipped out to leave a thin lining and then cooled to harden. Cream is then poured in and cooled before a thick layer of chocolate is poured over (enrobing) and allowed to cool and harden again. In 1902 Fry's Milk Chocolate was launched – later rechristened Fry's Five Boys. Orange Cream and Peppermint Cream followed with Fry's Five Centre in 1934

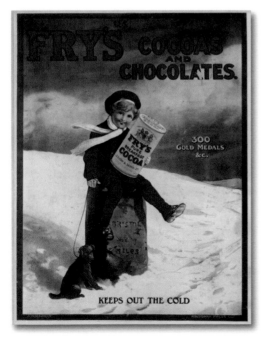

Fry's appealed to the younger market with this delightful advertisement.

(orange, raspberry, lime, strawberry and pineapple). Output of the cream bar exceeded half a million units per day at one point; the foil wrapping and blue label came in 1925.

Chocolate Cream was the first of many 'Specialties of the House', to be followed by Crunchie; Punch (in three flavours: Full Cream; Milk Chocolate; and Delicious Caramel and Milky Fudge); Caramets – produced in a pack 'ideal for both pocket and handbag'; Crunch Block; Turkish Delight ('exquisitely flavoured with genuine Otto of Roses'); and Five Boys.

Reproduction of three early advertisements of Walter Churchman's chocolate, the Patent Rights in which were purchased by Dr Joseph Fry.

Above: Pre-1832 Fry's advertisements for cocoa and chocolate; again, note the medical claims and the warnings against counterfeit products.

Above right: The Fry dynasty in the eighteenth and nineteenth centuries.

Right: Fry's cocoa was promoted as an ideal breakfast drink, good for children and recommended by doctors. Healthy-looking children start to appear in the advertisements.

In 1868 Fry's highly decorated chocolate boxes were launched, full of assorted chocolates: these were very popular at Christmas and sported a vast array of different coloured designs. The most sought after were the Double Milk Assortment (eleven different chocolates with a double milk chocolate coating); Sandwich Assortment (separated layers of milk and dark chocolate in one block); and Silver Lining Assortment (this contained Cherry in Fondant, Hazlenut Fudge and Fruit Nougatine). Market research was an important facet of Fry's marketing right from the start: the colour of the cups for these chocolates was chosen by 85 per cent of consumers.

By the 1870s Fry's could boast 220 different products, including the first British Easter egg in 1873. In 1902 it launched its first milk chocolate bar, five years after Cadbury's; its popular and enduring Fry's Turkish Bar came in 1914. In 1910 Fry's sponsored Captain Scott's expedition to Antarctica with a £1,000 donation, an early shrewd marketing move which elicited the following testimonial from Captain Scott:

> Messrs. J. S. Fry and Sons supplied our Cocoa, sledging and fancy chocolate, delicious comforts excellently packed and always in good condition … Crunching those elaborate chocolates brought one nearer to civilisation than anything we experienced sledging.

In the years leading up to the First World War, Fry's suffered badly from a lack of investment and its reputation declined as a result. In 1918 they merged with Cadbury to become The British Cocoa and Chocolate Company

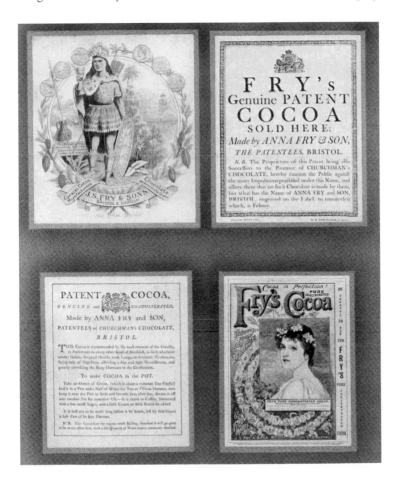

Early advertisements: (top left) the origins of the product are emphasised – Caracas beans and an Aztec; (top right) a caution against the 'felony' of counterfeiting; (bottom left) instructions on how to make chocolate; (bottom right) promotion of the solubility of Fry's product and an early example of the association of chocolate with beautiful women.

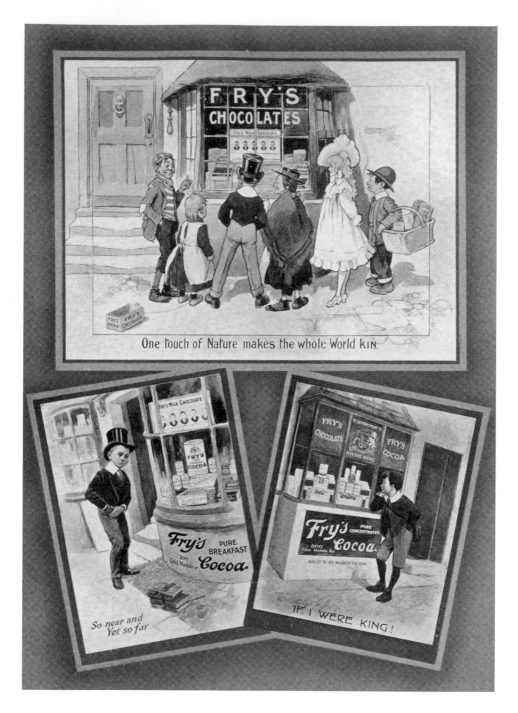

The 'Five Girls'
answer to the
famous 'Five Boys'
advertisement:
what is good for
the boys is good
for the girls.
The cow in the
background
reinforces the
health and purity
messages.

(Cadbury's value had been assessed as three times that of Fry's). Egbert (Bertie) Cadbury joined the Fry part of the business and he and Cecil Fry engineered the move to a purpose-built factory on 222 acres of countryside in Somerdale, Keynsham, in 1923, between the River Avon and the London–Bristol main line. Both companies retained their individual identities, marketing and branding of products. The new factory allowed them to mechanise production of fewer brands at a lower cost.

The move from Union Street was a gradual affair lasting twelve years until 1934, when six thousand people were on the payroll. The factory itself was set in parkland with poplar and chestnut trees, flower beds and lawns. *Fry's of Bristol*, an early corporate booklet, tells us that 'The Cocoa department looks on to woodland slopes and sunlit meadows', giving us a flavour of the bucolic setting of Somerdale.

Both the Fry and Cadbury families were Quakers and, like the Rowntrees in York, they were concerned to provide their workers with clean, safe and pleasant working conditions. The company employed a nurse and a doctor, ran 'continuation classes' (further education) for the girls, provided a gym with instructors, facilities and pitches for football, tennis, cricket and bowls and set up an operatic society, camera club, and debating and dramatic societies. Girls leaving to get married received a copy of *Mrs Beeton's Book of Household Management*.

Fry's characterises the inextricable connection of chocolate with Quakerism. Friends were excluded from the only teaching universities in England at the time, Oxford and Cambridge, because of the universities' affiliation to Anglicanism; they were debarred from Parliament; they were

Opposite:
Advertisements
aimed at tempting
children and
their parents:
(top) a claim that
chocolate fosters
friendship;
(bottom left)
the temptation
chocolate arouses
and the
importance of
saving up to make
that purchase;
(bottom right)
associations with
royalty and the
alleged aspirational
qualities of
chocolate. Note
the 'Five Boys'
advertisement
in two of the
confectionery
shop windows.

Fry's equivalent to the Royal Train – a specially fitted-out touring train providing valuable public relations for the company.

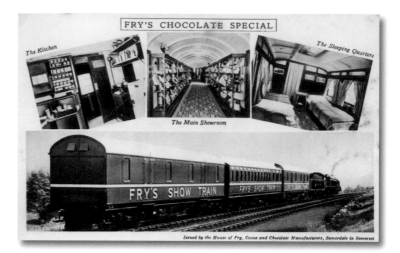

restricted in what they could and could not do as lawyers because they would not take oaths; and they were disqualified from the guilds and from the services because they were pacifists. One of the few alternatives left to a privileged and well-to-do young Quaker was a life in business. Moreover, cocoa and chocolate were attractive to Fry, Cadbury and Rowntree because of the attendant social benefits of a non-alcoholic beverage. Early concerns over the intrinsic insincerity of advertising and accusations of price-fixing and a Quaker chocolate

Chocolate refining at Fry's Somerdale factory.

Left: Fry's chocolate sellers at an early-twentieth-century football match. Note the insignia on the trays.

Below: The brave new world that greeted workers at Somerdale.

cartel were overcome to a greater or lesser degree, allowing the companies to get on with building a largely contented workforce, enlightened industrial relations, fair dealing and pleasant factories with an air of homeliness provided by potted plants and homely pictures on the factory walls. The provision of housing, entertainment, sport and education for employees was years ahead of its time, and managers routinely used workers' Christian names.

An early booklet, *Into the Open Country*, gives the company's mission statement and a flavour of the corporate ethos back then:

Fry's have kept before them two guiding principles: one, giving the public the best possible value in cocoa and chocolate manufactured under the best possible conditions; the other, of giving the workpeople the best facilities for recreation and happiness.

PUNCH, OR THE LONDON CHARIVARI—May 11, 1932

THE NEW IDEA

The New Idea in things delicious to eat and drink. The New Idea of how to make them. It was this reaching out for The New Idea that reared the world's most modern chocolate factory down here at Somerdale in

FRY'S
of Somerdale
in Somerset
•
Makers of chocolate as chocolate should be made

Somerset; that gave you Milk Chocolate made with British guaranteed pure milk; that gave you Fry's Malted Milk Cocoa with Eggs at a lower price than had been thought possible; and that *will* give you, before you are much older, the—but we'll keep that to ourselves for the present.

"IT'S AN ILL WIND THAT BLOWS NOBODY ANY GOOD."

CADBURY'S OF BOURNVILLE

T HE CADBURY STORY starts in 1824 with John Cadbury, son of a rich Quaker, selling non-alcoholic beverages – tea, coffee and sixteen varieties of drinking chocolate – at 93 Bull Street, Birmingham, after an apprenticeship in London at the Sanderson, Fox and Company teahouse. Soon after, Cadbury moved to a former malt house in Crooked Lane (where he perfected techniques of cacao-bean grinding to produce cocoa) and then to a factory in Bridge Street. John's brother Benjamin joined and the company became known as Cadbury Brothers of Birmingham. With an office in London and a Royal Warrant under its belt, the business benefited from the 1853 tax reduction on cocoa, enabling it to reduce retail prices and thus bring cocoa powder to a much wider market. As a consequence the sale of tea was abandoned in 1849 and left to nephew Richard Barrow Cadbury.

John Cadbury's sons, Richard and George, took over the business in 1861 – it was still very small with about ten employees and not at all successful. Competition was intense from Rowntree's, Fry's and companies such as Taylors in Spitalfields (manufacturers of more than fifty brands of cocoa and mustard) and Dunn & Hewett of Pentonville, who sold chocolate sticks, Patent Lentilised Chocolate (made from lentils, tapioca, sago or dried peas) and 'Plain Chocolate Sold in Drab Paper'.

Richard had joined their father soon after leaving school in 1851 while George followed in 1857 after a three-year apprenticeship with Rowntree's grocery business in Pavement in York. The rules of the shop there were uncompromising and set out in a memorandum written by Joseph Rowntree Senior:

> The object of the Pavement establishment is business. The young men who enter it … are expected to contribute … in making it successful … it affords a full opportunity for any painstaking, intelligent young man to obtain a good practical acquaintance with the tea and grocery trades … the place is not suitable for the indolent and wayward,

Opposite:
Tom Browne
Cadbury's
chocolate
advertisement
from 1906: 'It's an
ill wind that blows
nobody any good.'

The Bridge Street factory. Note how neatly the covered wagon fits through the archway. From an engraving by T. O. Barlow (RA) after a drawing by Henry Newman.

John Cadbury's tea dealership in Bull Street in Birmingham, c. 1830. Note the doves, symbolising Quaker pacifism, and the silk mercer next door, also a Cadbury. The Women's Mennonite Association are advertising a forthcoming meeting.

The 1862 Cadbury catalogue featured such brands as Chocolat du Mexique, Crystal Palace Chocolate, Dietetic Cocoa, Trinidad Rock Cocoa and Churchman's Cocoa. Cadbury produced the first chocolate box in 1868, full of chocolate candles and featuring Richard's daughter Jessica holding a kitten on the lid. Around the same time the firm produced the first Valentine's Day chocolate assortment. A pledge system was set up at the factory whereby a penny was awarded to any worker who had not succumbed to the temptation of eating the manufactured product during the week.

An 1847 family photograph of John Cadbury and his family.

By 1878 it was becoming increasingly necessary to find a site which facilitated the importation of cocoa and milk and allowed them to mechanise appropriately; the 14.5-acre Georgian Bournbrook Hall and Estate, 5 miles south of the city centre, fitted the bill with its easy access to the Birmingham West Suburban Railway and the Worcester and Birmingham Canal. This was duly purchased and Bournville, with its

The comprehensive production, packaging and transportation processes at Bournville, as depicted in the Cadbury archive.

➡ COCOA BEANS & PLAIN CHOCOLATE	➡ WRAPPERS & CARTONS
➡ CHOCOLATE WITH MILK & SUGAR ADDED	

FROM COCOA BEAN TO CHOCOLATE BAR *By following the black arrows, then the red and the green, you may trace the various stages of manufacture and assembly through the factory to the point of despatch.*

BOATS BRINGING FRESH MILK FOR CADBURY'S MILK CHOCOLATE.
There are 1½ glasses of fresh full cream milk in every ½-lb. of Cadbury's Milk Chocolate.

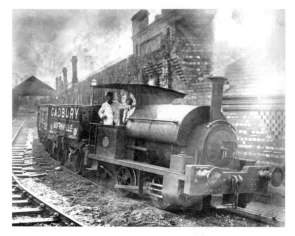

Above: Barges on the canal transporting churns of fresh milk from Knighton or Frampton-on-Severn to Bournville (the canal shipments transferred to rail in 1928).

Above right: A Cadbury locomotive hauling some open wagons inside the works, c. 1912.

French (and therefore fashionable) overtones, was adopted as the name for the site for the opening in 1879.

Cadbury soon had a fleet of barges working the canal, in Cadbury livery, and was the first company to use powered canal boats. By the turn of the century sidings were built to link the factory with the national railway network and Cadbury rolling stock was manufactured. Horse-drawn vans were its earliest mode of road transport. In the 1920s the factory was reconstructed and the site expanded to cope with demand and new production techniques. Until the 1960s all the affiliated crafts and trades required to run a chocolate manufacturing plant were carried out on site – these included the manufacture of boxes, cartons and tin cans, machine making, sheet metal production, printing, joinery, advertising and marketing.

But it was not all about the factory. A further 120 acres had been bought by George in 1893 and a model village built to 'alleviate the evils of more modern cramped living conditions'. This visionary achievement was inspired by what George could see all around him in central Birmingham:

> It is not easy to describe or imagine the dreary desolation which acre after acre of the very heart of the town presents ... hundreds of leaky, damp, wretched houses, wholly unfit for human habitation.

Within seven years the new village comprised 313 sound, clean and sanitary houses (complete with front and back gardens) on 330 acres of land. Residents were provided with a booklet laying down rules for keeping houses and gardens in good order, abstaining from alcohol on the Sabbath, and the advantages of single beds for married couples. The area was alcohol-free,

An early form of alfresco office aerobics, complete with piano;

with no pubs and no alcohol sold in local shops, until a licensed members' bar opened in the Rowheath Pavilion in 1940. This abstinence was a reflection of John Cadbury's strict Temperance beliefs and a manifestation of his work in social reform, which also included campaigns for workhouse reform and against industrial pollution, child labour (particularly child chimney sweeps), and animal cruelty.

Cadbury was one of the first companies in Britain to introduce half-day holidays. Philanthropy and paternalism continued in the workplace with ground breaking pension schemes, a sick club, medical services, outings, in-service education, staff committees (the Works Councils) and reasonable

Popular staff swimming lessons, 1910.

Physical education at the Bournville PE den in 1902.

wages. George and Richard Cadbury were fervent believers in the value of education – they both taught at the Birmingham Adult Schools – and this was maintained at Bournville where continuation classes were set up in 1913 to provide free further education (during working hours) for younger employees from when they left school and joined Cadbury aged fourteen until they were sixteen, later extended to eighteen. A wide range of

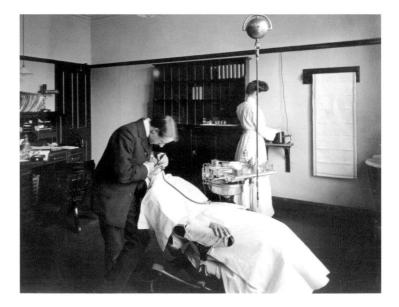

The first company dentist, Dr J. Jenkins Robb MD, shown here in his surgery, converted from one of the workers' cottages near to No. 2 Lodge (1905).

apprenticeships was established for the boys and a sewing club for the girls. Employees were, as a matter of course, treated with respect. The Works Councils, segregated until 1964, worked in concert with the trades unions, which had also always been encouraged; the councils were made up of management and shop floor representatives and were primarily responsible for the company's welfare schemes.

In common with other factories of the time, male and female workers were segregated with separate entrances, working, rest and dining areas and Works Councils. Technicians going into women's areas of the factory had to wear armbands showing that they had permission to be there. Married women were prohibited and girls had to leave on marriage – but not before they were presented with a Bible and a carnation and a talk from one of the directors. It was not until the shortage of male workers caused by the Second World War that married women began to be recruited.

Social and recreational facilities were a vital part of the Cadbury community: land was bought at Rowheath for football and hockey pitches and a running track. The pavilion opened in 1924 not just as a clubhouse and changing facility for the sportsmen and women but also as a venue for dinners and dances. In addition, there were bowling greens, a fishing lake and an outdoor lido. An indoor swimming pool was built in Bournville Lane; a boating lake and the cricket pitch made famous on the Milk Tray boxes followed – all the sports facilities were free of charge.

Meanwhile, back on the production line things were not going well – that is, until George's 1866 visit to Van Houten to acquire a press; this visit was pivotal and enabled a company on the verge of failure to be transformed into the successful company it soon became. Eschewing Quaker reservations about advertising, the Cadburys set about gaining medical testimonials and establishing the health-giving credentials of their products. Both the *British Medical Journal* and *The Lancet* gave their approval to Cocoa Essence when it was launched in late 1866, the former asserting it to be 'one of the most nutritious, digestible and restorative drinks'. *The Grocer* magazine joined in the praise, emphasising the absence of adulteration; the advertising campaign devised to capitalise on these endorsements featured the slogan 'Absolutely Pure, Therefore Best. No Chemicals Used.'

The testimonial from *The Lancet*, 27 July 1867.

Guaranteed Genuine.

OPINIONS OF THE
MEDICAL PRESS

From the LANCET, July 27, 1867.

"Genuine Cocoa consists to the extent of about one-half of fatty matter or butter of Cocoa, as it has been termed. The presence of this in amount so large renders pure and unmixed Cocoa too rich for some stomachs; but since the majority of the preparations of Cocoa met with in the shops are not genuine, but consist of mixtures of cocoa, sugar, and starch, the objection of richness can seldom be made. The Cocoa to which Messrs. Cadbury Brothers have given the name of 'Cocoa Essence,' professes to be free from both sugar and added starch, and to consist of the cocoa bean reduced to powder from which about two-thirds of the fatty matter or butter have been removed; the richness is thus overcome in a manner far preferable to the impoverishment of the Cocoa by dilution or adulteration. We have examined the samples brought under our notice, and find that they are genuine, and that the Essence of Cocoa is just what it is declared to be by Messrs. Cadbury Brothers."

The purity
message was
vital to the success
of Cadbury's
cocoa, as this
advertisement
shows ('Absolute
freedom from
alkaline
adulteration').
Testimonials from
The Lancet and
The Analyst are
cited: 'the typical
cocoa of English
manufacture ...
absolutely pure'.

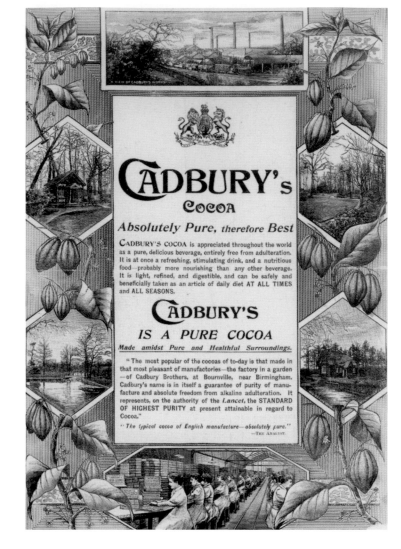

The early 1870s saw the launch of the exotic and luxurious, decidedly un-Quakerly, French-influenced Fancy Box, complete with silk lining and mirror – the *Chemist & Druggist* described it as 'Divine'. The most exquisite chocolate ever to come under our notice.' Easter eggs were introduced in 1875 and Cadbury Fingers in 1897.

The famous chocolatièr Frederic Kinchelman joined the company, bringing with him his successful recipes and production techniques for Nougat-Dragées, Pâte Duchesse and Avelines. One of its new brands was

named 'The Model Parish Cocoa' in anticipation of the model village to be built at Bournville.

The new technology and expertise in recipes led to the successful production of chocolate bars and, in 1898, milk chocolate bars made with Daniel Peter's powdered milk technique, soon to be replaced in 1905 with fresh milk. This manifested itself in Cadbury's Dairy Milk – a successful challenge to the popular Swiss milk chocolate bars. The original plan was to call it 'Dairy Maid' but the name was changed at the last minute after the daughter of a customer in Plymouth remarked that Dairy Milk was a 'much daintier name'. Bournville Cocoa was launched a year later.

From 1905 the roll call of new Cadbury chocolate products is nothing short of breathtaking. Dairy Milk on its launch contained more milk than other chocolate bars ('a glass and a half of fresh milk') and became the top-selling brand by 1913. Cadbury had overtaken Fry as the biggest UK manufacturer in 1910 with sales of £1,670,221 compared with Fry's £1,642,715 and Rowntree's £1,200,598. The year 1915 saw the debut of Milk Tray – originally presented in open boxes on wooden trays (hence the name) – followed by Flake, made from folds of milk chocolate, in 1920 ('the crumbliest, flakiest milk chocolate in the world'). Milk Tray packaging has changed almost imperceptibly since then and still sells over 8 million boxes every year. The familiar purple packaging was introduced on Dairy Milk in 1920, the colour

The focus of the two advertisements above is on the fortifying benefits to growing children and on nourishment for adults ('makes strong men stronger').

A splendid parade of Cadbury motor delivery vans and their proud drivers at the London depot in the late 1920s.

chosen for its noble connotations going back to the Roman senatorial classes and the emperors. The famous Cadbury signature started life in 1921.

Creme Eggs were introduced in 1923, and today 66,000 eggs are 'laid' every hour. Crunchie and Fruit & Nut arrived in 1929 and Whole Nut hit the market in 1933. Cadbury's Roses selection arrived in 1938 and its distinctive 'Dorothy bag' carton was introduced in 1946 – annual production today exceeds 13,000 tonnes.

This 1927 advertisement was designed to appeal to fashionable young women.

Below: Cadbury's Roses assortments in their iconic 'Dorothy bag' cartons over the years.

Opposite: A sea, road and rail transport poster, 1925. Like so many advertisements of the era, it uses depictions of the most modern forms of transport to convey the reach of the company.

ROWNTREE'S OF YORK

EANWHILE, 104 miles to the north-east, a remarkably similar story to
that of Cadbury had been unfolding. It begins with Mary Tuke, who came
from a famous Quaker family and whose grandfather was jailed for his non-
conformism in the 1660s. In 1725, aged thirty, Mary established a grocery
business in York, first in Walmgate, then Castlegate, and, after a number of legal
wrangles with York Merchant Adventurers' Company, finally won the right to
trade as a grocer in 1732. She was joined in 1746 by her nephew William, who
inherited the business on Mary's death in 1752. The shop specialised in the sale
of coffee, chicory and drinking chocolate. When William's son Henry joined the
business in 1785, they began to sell tea and to manufacture cocoa and chocolate
themselves. Henry's grandson, Samuel, was a good friend of fellow Quaker
Joseph Rowntree I, as well as being related to him through marriage. Joseph
too was a grocer with a shop in Pavement, York.

In July 1862 Joseph's son, Henry Isaac Rowntree (who had served his
apprenticeship both at the family shop in Pavement and at Tuke's), bought
the Tukes' business. The firm was relatively small, with about twelve staff
and sales of about £3,000 – 10 per cent of Cadbury sales and 5 per cent of
Fry sales at the time. The bulk of the output was Tuke's Superior Cocoa, later
to become Rowntree's Prize Medal Rock Cocoa – this was made, using pre-
Van Houten technology, into fine ground cakes but suffered from the oiliness
characteristic of the manufacturing process.

Henry relocated the firm to an old foundry at Tanner's Moat in 1864;
however, the combination of Henry's preoccupation with Quaker-related
activities, old technology and small-scale, short-run manufacturing
techniques compromised any real progress and, like Cadbury's at the time,
the business was ailing. In 1869 he was joined by his brother, Joseph
Rowntree II, and the firm H. I. Rowntree & Co. was established. Joseph
brought much-needed business acumen to the company and focused on the
financial and sales side, leaving the manufacturing to Henry; in effect he
probably saved the 'hopelessly embarrassed' company from bankruptcy,
bailing out a brother who 'knew next to nothing of the business'.

Opposite:
Scene from Joe
Dickinson's
unique 'museum'
of Rowntree's
memorabilia –
probably the
biggest repository
of Rowntree's
artefacts and
marketing
materials in the
world. The ten
thousand artefacts
are kept in a house
in York entirely
given over to
Rowntree's
products.

Advertisement for prize-winning Rock Cocoa from the turn of the twentieth century, emphasising its purity.

The Tanner's Moat and North Street factory on the River Ouse at York.

Poster advertising Elect Cocoa, conspicuous for its prize competition and testimonial from *The Lancet*.

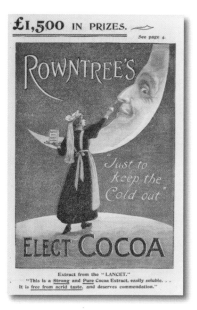

A combination of Joseph's meticulousness, increased product lines and a rise in demand revived the company's fortunes. This was of course also helped by market trends: indeed, between 1870 and 1890 cocoa consumption in the United Kingdom increased from nearly 7,000,000lb to over 20,000,000lb with a rise in consumption per capita from 0.22lb to 0.53lb. In 1876, Homoeopathic Cocoa was launched, riding on the popularity of the medicinal content allegedly provided by arrowroot. Other products included Iceland Moss, Flake Cocoa, Chocolate Creams, Chocolate Balls, Chocolate Beans and Chocolate Drops.

But while others were embracing marketing and advertising in the chocolate and other industries, Joseph had a problem with advertising (or 'puffery', as he called it). He preferred to let the quality of his cocoa speak for itself, delivering goods to wholesalers and retailers unbranded and, indeed, bearing the name of the customer rather than 'Rowntree'. To Joseph, as with some other Quakers and to some extent shopkeeper-manufacturers generally, advertising smacked of disingenuousness and implied substandard goods. The result was that none of Rowntree's lines was particularly successful and although between 1870 and 1879 sales rose from £7,384 to £30,890, margins remained tight and losses were recorded in 1873 and 1876. Only four out of nineteen lines turned a profit although these did account for 70 per cent of sales.

As we have seen, the Quakers' belief in the value of the individual led to a paternalistic and fair, virtually non-hierarchical relationship with their workers; their innate pacifism eschewed confrontation with the workforce and generated a preoccupation with the welfare of their employees which extended to social activities, sick pay, loans and pensions of sorts. Mutual trust and respect were the order of the day, extending, at Rowntree's, even to staff logging their hours worked themselves.

A sales call by Claude Gaget in 1879 had a significant impact on Rowntree's. Gaget was working out of the London office of Compagnie Française, Parisian confectioners. The samples of gums and pastilles he presented that day eventually led to the manufacture in 1881 (but only when the finished product was perfected and of the highest quality) of Rowntree's famous Crystallized Gum Pastilles in 4lb unbranded wooden boxes. An immediate success, sales of the pastilles enabled the company to expand into premises in North Street adjacent to Tanner's Moat. By 1885, 4 tonnes were produced weekly; these sweets were the precursors of Rowntree's Fruit Gums and Fruit Pastilles.

Henry Rowntree's death in 1883 led to Joseph's two sons joining the firm: John Wilhelm in 1885 and Benjamin Seebohm in 1888; Seebohm established the company's first laboratory. The dramatic expansion in

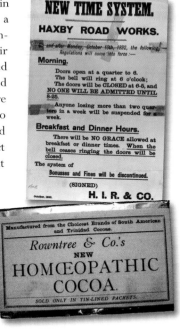

NEW TIME SYSTEM.

HAXBY ROAD WORKS.

On and after Monday, October 10th, 1892, the following Regulations will come into force :—

Morning.

Doors open at a quarter to 6.
The bell will ring at 6 o'clock;
The doors will be CLOSED at 6-5, and NO ONE WILL BE ADMITTED UNTIL 8-25.

Anyone losing more than two quarters in a week will be suspended for a week.

Breakfast and Dinner Hours.

There will be NO GRACE allowed at breakfast or dinner times. When the bell ceases ringing the doors will be closed.

The system of Bonusses and Fines will be discontinued.

(SIGNED)

H. I. R. & CO.

Manufactured from the Choicest Brands of South American and Trinidad Cocoas.

Rowntree & Co.'s
NEW
HOMŒOPATHIC
COCOA.

SOLD ONLY IN TIN-LINED PACKETS.

Left: Staff notice at Rowntree's (1892) demonstrating how important good attendance and punctuality were to the Rowntrees; its paternalism was truly impressive but staff had to earn it.

Left: Homoeopathic Cocoa, trading on the alleged medicinal qualities of cocoa containing arrowroot.

Below left: Rowntree's packers in the late nineteenth century.

Below right: An image of the poverty in Hungate, York, which the Rowntrees were determined to alleviate. Note the privy on the left.

Packers busy completing a consignment destined for Natal and South Africa – gifts from Queen Victoria to her subjects.

consumption of cocoa during these years was reflected in Rowntree's sales: between 1870 and 1890 they grew from £7,384 to £114,529, increasing to £463,199 in 1900. In 1870 Rowntree's had 4 per cent of the UK market, increasing to 15 per cent by 1900, while Cadbury was at 27 per cent in 1870 rising to 41 per cent in 1900. All of this was at the expense of Fry, whose share declined from 70 per cent to 44 per cent over the same period.

The success of Fruit Pastilles and Fruit Gums enabled Joseph to invest in new machinery in 1880, notably a Van Houten press for the production in York of cocoa essence – Rowntree's Elect, 'more than a drink, a food', was made from top-quality cocoa. Despite the new technology and increased demand, however, output remained low (in 1893 Elect still only accounted for 6 per cent of sales and 2.5 per cent of output); company profits were unimpressive at 2.5 per cent of turnover in 1888. Notwithstanding, and no doubt with an eye on Cadbury's achievements at Bournville, in 1890 Joseph

Part of the manufacturing process at Rowntree's.

bought a 20-acre site to the north of the city centre on Haxby Road with a view to building a more efficient and ergonomic factory which would enable the firm to meet the growing demand for its products. The factory had its own railway line and halt and by 1898 all production was on the new site. The number of employees in 1884 was 182; by 1899 this had risen to 1,613. Fry and Cadbury had seen equally dramatic increases over a similar period. The 1890s saw the Rowntree's sales force increase from fourteen in 1890 to thirty-three in 1897. Shop displays were increasing but advertising was still minimal despite the fact that the other players in the market – Fry, Cadbury, Van Houten and Cailler – were all advertising their products aggressively, and it was not until 1897 that Rowntree's embarked on a cohesive and resourced marketing campaign for Rowntree's Elect Cocoa.

On the social side, Joseph Rowntree followed his Quaker instincts by establishing the Joseph Rowntree Trusts and beginning the building of New Earswick at the turn of the century. The objective was to provide the worker of even the lowest means with a new type of house that was clean, sanitary and efficient. Rowntree's deep concern for the welfare of his workers, the research findings of his son, Seebohm, into the plight of the urban poor, his own Quaker beliefs, Cadbury's achievements at Bournville and the pioneering work on garden cities by Ebenezer Howard – all of these factors combined to drive the establishment of New Earswick just north of the city of York and minutes away from the Haxby Road factory.

For the next thirty years or so the company languished in the doldrums. The Depression, a lack of clear policy, a tendency to produce a lot of short-run unprofitable lines, the failure to compete with Cadbury's Dairy Milk and the persistent suspicion of advertising and marketing all contributed. They bought into Gray, Dunn (boiled sweet and chocolate

An aerial view of the Haxby Road factory with biplane and endorsement by HRH the Prince of Wales, 31 May 1923.

AERIAL VIEW OF
ROWNTREE'S COCOA AND CHOCOLATE WORKS

THE FACTORY ESTATE COVERS 222 ACRES
THE EMPLOYEES NUMBER MORE THAN 7,000

"Surely this is one of the biggest factories in the World"

HRH THE PRINCE OF WALES
May 31st 1923

45

Right: Delivering
Rowntree's goods
in Zululand.

The unmistakable
Plain Mr York,
drawn by Alfred
Leete, promoting
Rowntree's
Motoring
Chocolate; a very
familiar sight in the
1920s. Motoring
Chocolate was
launched in 1926
and came to the
end of the road in
1964. As well as
getting a box of
chocolates, visitors
to the York factory
also received a
booklet entitled
'A Walk and a Talk
with Mr York'.

AN "OVERSEAS SPECIAL" IN ZULULAND.

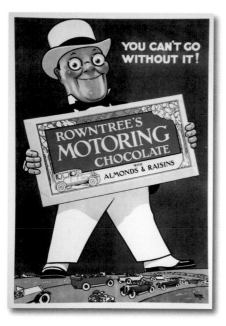

biscuit manufacturers) in 1924 and launched Plain York Chocolate bar the
following year (promoted with the repetitious slogan 'Plain Mr York of
York, Yorkshire'). The fruit and nut block Motoring followed in 1925, while
unsuccessful overtures were made to take over neighbours Cravens,
chocolate and confectionery manufacturers. York Milk was launched in
1927 but this suffered against Cadbury's Dairy
Milk because it was made from powdered milk and
had none of the taste and health advantages of the
aggressively advertised and marketed 'glass and a
half' milk chocolate bar. Tried Favourites came in
1927 but these assortments faced strong
competition from Rowntree's York neighbours,
Terry's. That same year they bought into the
chewing gum market by joining forces with US
manufacturer Beech Nut.

It was, however, the appointment and
subsequent rise of sales manager, marketing director
and future chairman George Harris which began to
make a real difference. Harris' experience of
American marketing methods, product
development, branding and advertising eventually
led to the change from a conservative, production-
led company to a market-driven one, ultimately
resulting in the launch of KitKat, Black Magic, Aero,
Dairy Box, Smarties, Rolos and Polos in the 1930s.

Attempts in 1931 to form an alliance with Halifax toffee firm Mackintosh came to nothing for Rowntree's but it did lead to Harold Mackintosh's purchase of Caley from Unilever. By now, however, the focus was on producing a competitor to Dairy Milk and this gave birth to Extra Creamy Milk in 1933. On the chocolate assortment front, Black Magic was launched in 1933, 'the first chocolate assortment ever made to order for a mass market'. Market research was, at last, being embraced: the number of chocolates in Black Magic boxes (twelve) was decided on after interviews with 2,500 shopkeepers and seven thousand consumers. Also of significance is the fact that the company name was sacrificed in favour of the Black Magic brand name. The hard, soft and praline centres were aimed squarely at the best-selling assortment box of the day, Cadbury's King George Assortment. However, the Dairy Milk competitor, Extra Creamy Milk, flopped soon after it was launched in 1933.

It was Aero, an aerated rather than a solid chocolate, which provided the first real success for Rowntree's in 1935 and soon started to eat into Dairy Milk's market share. At the same time Wafer Crisp, later Chocolate Crisp, later KitKat, hit the shops – sold with the slogan 'Give yourself a break at tea time' and launched on a meagre budget of £1,750. The simple, enduring rationale behind it was to produce 'a chocolate bar that a man could take to work in his pack up' – an idea from a Rowntree's employee. The name had first appeared on a box of assorted chocolates in the 1920s (it had been trademarked in 1911) and derived from the eighteenth-century Whig literary club, whose proprietor, pie shop owner Christopher Catling ('Kit Cat'), featured on the box. In 1931 the Kit Cat assortment was a casualty of a product review.

Dairy Box was launched in 1936 against Milk Tray, and Blue Riband reached the shops in 1937. Chocolate Beans, later Smarties, followed in 1938 – originally sold loose but later in their iconic tubes – and were an imitation of the already established French dragée. The famous letter stamped on the cap as 'an attractive plaything for children' was introduced in 1959. On the confectionery side, Polo mints were launched in 1939, based on the American Lifesaver sweet; Polo fruits followed in 1953.

An early KitKat-Chocolate Crisp advertisement emphasising the 'snack' factor.

An Aero advertisement from around 1955.

47

Terry's
THISTLE
CHOCOLATE ASSORTMENT

APRICOT CARDINAL

PRALINE CUP

JAMAICA CREAM

TRUFFLE NONPAREILS

RUSSIAN CARAMEL

BULLION DESSERT

CHAMPAGNE CORK

TRUFFLE BRICK

BITTER CHOCOLATE PASTILLE

MARZIPAN BOUCHÉE

MOCCA DESSERT

TERRY'S OF YORK

O N THE OTHER SIDE of York from Rowntree's, Joseph Terry had been making cocoa and chocolate since 1886 and by the end of the 1920s had become the market leader in chocolate assortments. Joseph Terry came to York from nearby Pocklington, where he was born in 1793, to serve an apprenticeship to an apothecary in Stonegate. An advertisement in *The York Courant* in 1813 proclaims that he is established 'opposite the Castle, selling spices, pickling vinegar, essence of spruce, patent medicines and perfumery' – the usual trade for an apothecary. Later, he moved this chemist's shop to Walmgate. In 1823 he married Harriet Atkinson, a relative of Robert Berry, who ran a small confectionery business with William Bayldon near Bootham Bar; Terry gave up being a chemist and druggist and joined Berry in St Helen's Square. George Berry succeeded his father to form Terry & Berry but George left in 1826, leaving Joseph to develop what then was essentially a confectionery business.

By 1840 Joseph Terry's products were being delivered to seventy-five towns all over England: they included candied eringo (the preserved root of sea-holly and an aphrodisiac); coltsfoot rock (a hardened stick of brittle rock candy flavoured with coltsfoot, a plant with hoof-shaped leaves); gum balls and lozenges made from squill (the bulb of the sea onion, often used as an expectorant); camphor (an aromatic compound traditionally used in mothballs and creams to reduce itching); and horehound (a member of the mint family used to soothe sore throats, stimulate the appetite, and as a relief for flatulence). Apart from boiled sweets, they also made marmalade, marzipan, mushroom ketchup and calves' jelly. Conversation lozenges, the precursors of Love Hearts (with such risqué slogans as 'Can you polka?', 'I want a wife', 'Do you love me?' and 'How do you flirt?') were particularly popular. Chocolate production had begun in earnest in around 1867 with thirteen chocolate products (including chocolate creams and batons) adding to the other 380 or so confectionery and parfait lines. These included, for example, bismuth and lavender lozenges, acidulated drops, Indian sugar sticks, toffee tablets, apricots in syrup, *pâte de jujubes* and chocolate cigars. Without doubt this was a list aimed squarely at the better-off in late Victorian society.

Opposite:
A selection of
Terry's products
from an early
trade catalogue.

On his death in 1850, Joseph Terry left the business to his son, Joseph Junior, then aged twenty-two. In 1864 young Joseph leased a riverside factory at Clementhorpe on the River Ouse, affording warehousing space and access to the Humber estuary and the North Sea; this in turn, along with the railways, facilitated both the importation of sugar, cocoa, other ingredients and the coal required for the steam-powered machinery, and the export of finished products.

The St Helen's Square premises were retained and converted into a fine shop, ballroom and restaurant; you can still see the Terry name on the building's facia and on

NEAPOLITANS
4d. and 3d. each
CROQUETTES
4d. each

MILK CHOCOLATE

Above: Distinctive chocolate 'boxes' in a variety of shapes and sizes.

Right: A selection of Terry's products from an early trade catalogue, including the Chocolate Apple and the famous Chocolate Orange.

Opposite page: A selection of Terry's famous dark and bitter chocolates: note the emphasis on French branding.

DESSERT CHOCOLATE APPLE
2/- each

SPARTAN BARREL
2/- each

DESSERT CHOCOLATE ORANGE
2/- each

CROQUETTES. - Nom. 3 oz. 1/- per packet.

LANGUES DE CHAT.
In 2 sizes Nom. 8 oz. and 4 oz. 3/- & 1/6 per box.

PASTILLES.
In 2 sizes Nom. 8 oz. and 4 oz. 3/- & 1/6 per box.

CAKES.
In 2 sizes Nom. 8 oz. and 4 oz. 2/6 & 1/3 per cake.

NEAPOLITANS. - In 2 sizes. 1/- & 6d. per packet.

An impressive window display at Terry's shop and restaurant in St Helen's Square, York. The building still exists and displays the Terry name on the metal window ledges and on the facia. Betty's Tea Rooms continues to thrive directly opposite today.

the brass window ledges. Joseph Junior died in 1898 and was succeeded by his sons Thomas Walker Leaper Terry and Frank Terry. The famous Neapolitans brand was launched in 1899, and early twentieth-century chocolate products included Britannia Assortment, York Milk Chocolates and Empire Mixture. Just before the First World War Frank made an important trip to Germany, bringing back production techniques and equipment to York. Up to the Second World War, Theatre Chocolates were available with their unique rustle-proof wrappers.

Terry's factory in Bishopthorpe Road, York.

In 1926, under the auspices of Frank and Noel Terry (Thomas's son), the company moved again, to the purpose-built Chocolate Works in Bishopthorpe Road, which still stands today. The site covers 14 acres and the tower is 135 feet high. Between the years 1918 and 1938 revenue doubled, and the number of employees stood at 2,500 in 1937, 60 per cent of whom were women. These increases were due in part to the launch in 1932 of All Gold and Chocolate Orange. The famous Chocolate Orange started life as the Chocolate Apple (phased out in 1954) and at one point one in ten Christmas stockings reputedly contained a Terry's Chocolate Orange.

Left: A Terry's poster with a typically coy girl doing the promoting.

Above: Modern wrapper for the famous Terry's Chocolate Orange.

Below: Terry's price list and a selection of early products: some appealed to the exotic; others to the wholesomeness associated with Devon milk.

OTHER BRITISH CHOCOLATE MANUFACTURERS

I N ADDITION to the four companies described above, a number of smaller British manufacturers made sure that the 'A' companies, as they became known, did not have it all their own way.

CALEY'S, NORWICH

In 1857 Albert Jarman Caley opened a chemist's business in London Street, Norwich, became famous for his mineral waters and soft drinks, and in 1883 began to make drinking chocolate, followed by eating chocolate three years later. In 1898 the manufacture of Christmas crackers began and A. J. Caley & Sons Ltd was formed. Caley's London chocolate showroom was in Bishopsgate Street. To compete with Swiss imports, Caley insisted on the best milk and drew its supplies from the famous Whitlingham herd of red poll cattle. An early description of the packing department tells us that 'the girls … are all dressed in neat striped print uniforms, and they look quite picturesque while working.'

John Mackintosh & Sons Ltd of Halifax acquired Caley's in 1932 although the Caley's brand name continued to be used until the early 1960s. A Royal Warrant was granted by Queen Mary in 1932 and 1941 saw the first manufacture of 'Cocoa Rich' Milk Marching Chocolate.

In 1942 Caley's Norwich factory was destroyed by the Luftwaffe in the Baedeker raids but it reopened after rebuilding in 1947; production of Caley lines had in the meantime been moved to Halifax. In 1969 Mackintosh merged with Rowntree's to form Rowntree Mackintosh, which was acquired by Nestlé in 1988. The Norwich factory closed in 1994 and in 1996 three former executives acquired Caley's brands and production equipment from Nestlé and formed Caley's of Norwich Ltd. In 1997 Caley's Plain Marching Chocolate was relaunched and in 1998 Caley's Milk Marching Chocolate was reintroduced.

The Caley name lives on in Norwich – since 2002 the fifteenth-century Guildhall has been home to Caley's Cocoa Café – a traditionally styled tea-room with the history of Caley's depicted around the walls. Today Caley

Opposite:
A 1953 advertisement from *Punch*, one of many striking images used by Caley.

Right: Poster showing an impressive Caley trade stand from the early twentieth century.

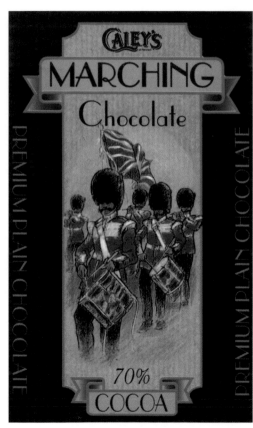

Above: Caley associating with things French and Swiss in an early advertisement, complete with yodelling milkmaids and milk-producing cow.

Left: Caley's famous Marching Chocolate is currently on the march again, available by the case in three varieties from its website.

markets its Fairtrade chocolates and hot drinks from its website and since 2008 it has been partners with Help for Heroes, selling, among other products, the revived Marching Chocolate. In 2010 a second Cocoa Café opened in Norwich's White Lion Street.

TUNNOCK'S, UDDINGSTON

Thomas Tunnock established Tunnock's in 1890 when he bought a baker's shop in Uddingston, south of Glasgow, for £80. The firm quickly became a Scottish institution and today still enjoys something of a cult market. Its famous Teacakes, Tunnock's Chocolate Caramel Wafer, Caramel Logs and Snowballs have been produced since the 1950s. Oddly, Tunnock's Teacake is not really a tea cake: it is in fact a round shortbread biscuit covered in a marshmallow-like mixture, itself covered in milk or dark chocolate. The Caramel Wafer is a bar consisting of five layers of wafer, interlaid with four layers of caramel and all coated in chocolate made with condensed milk. The wrappers of the milk chocolate version tell us that 'more than 5,000,000 of these biscuits [are] made and sold every week'. The Snowball is similar to the Teacake, with the addition of grated coconut to the exterior of a soft chocolate shell but with no biscuit base.

Women in the Tunnock's factory in the 1950s preparing wafers.

Tunnock's can count among its fan club the Sultana of Brunei, who came with her entourage to the factory to enjoy one of the regular tours. St Andrew's University runs a Tunnock's Caramel Wafer Appreciation Society, which is one of the oldest student societies at the university. The trademark face of the Tunnock's Boy was chosen by Thomas Tunnock because of the fresh, friendly image his face brought to the business. Indeed, 'You can't top a Tunnock's!'

Above: Tunnock's products on the move down the M8 motorway.

Wafer cutting at Tunnock's in the 1960s.

THORNTONS, SHEFFIELD

The company was established by Joseph William Thornton in 1911 when he left his job as a sales representative for the Don Confectionery Company and opened his first Thorntons Chocolate Kabin shop on the corner of Norfolk Street and Howard Street in Sheffield. He sold a wide range of confectionery including Kunzle cakes, Mackintosh toffee, Violet Cachous, Sweet-Lips, Phul-Nanas and Curiously Strong Mints. Chocolate production began in 1913 in the back room of his second shop on The Moor. When Joseph William died in 1919 his sons Norman and Stanley took over the business and formed J. W. Thornton Ltd. Easter eggs and Thorntons Special Toffee were the main lines until the 1950s, when the Continental Chocolates range was launched.

In 1948 the company moved to a factory in Belper and in 1954 Walter Willen, a Swiss confectioner, joined Thorntons and created a range of handmade confectionery called 'Swiss Assortment'; the name was changed to 'Continental Assortment', after complaints from the Swiss Embassy. Another new factory opened in Alfreton in 1985. Thorntons today turns over £215 million with four hundred shops and cafes and around two hundred franchises, together with Internet and mail order services. After the takeover of Cadbury's by Kraft, Thorntons became the largest independent chocolate and confectionery company in the United Kingdom.

The packing department at Elizabeth Shaw, the company which evolved from Packer, in the 1960s.

PACKER & CO., BRISTOL

H.J. Packer, a former Fry's employee, began trading in 1881, making chocolate from his house in Armoury Square, Bristol, under the name of Packer & Co. The workforce was Packer's sister and brother, and a Miss Lily Brown, who was paid 2s 6d a week; the plant comprised a kitchen fire and a paraffin lamp, two saucepans and a small pan for making the chocolate and the cream centres. Sugar was bought in 14lb loads and the finished chocolates were delivered by hand. In 1884 Packer took on H. J. Burrows – another ex-Fry's employee – and when the partnership was dissolved in 1885 it was Burrows who took over the business. The next year saw the 24 year old Bruce Cole pay Burrows £950 for all plant, stock, debts and goodwill.

Making the caramel at Packer's in the 1920s.

Carsons
LIMITED
SHORTWOOD · BRISTOL
Telephone: Bristol 65-3211

Christmas 1959

Above
14 oz. Mascot 4/-
Packed in ½ dozens

AMBASSADOR

Ambassador
3 lb. — 27/6
2 lb. — 18/6
Packed in singles

Above
1 lb. Ambassador 8/6
Packed in ¼ dozens

Above
6 lb. Presentation Box
'Ambassador' Chocolates 60/-
Packed in singles

A selection of prestigious assortment boxes from Elizabeth Shaw's Carson brand, Christmas 1959.

Business began to boom from 1896 and in 1901 the company moved to a specially commissioned, high specification factory at Greenbank. The business grew further and between 1903 and 1912 sales increased by 250 per cent. Its strategy to sell 'Two Ounces a Penny' chocolate – good quality chocolates at a price a child could afford – had taken off. Packer's Chocolate Mixtures was one of its main lines.

In *c.* 1908 they purchased Carson's Ltd, a high-quality confectionery firm based in Glasgow. To extend its range, the company launched a new subsidiary to produce high-class chocolates like the 'walnut whirl': and so Bond's of Bristol chocolate products began to be produced on new production lines in the Greenbank factory alongside the Packer's brands. Success continued into the early 1920s, with the company employing 2,500 workers at its peak.

The end of the First World War saw a return of the low-cost Packer's brand at a penny an ounce. One of the new lines, Milk Crispets, was particularly popular and went on to become the company's most enduring product. By 1922 Packers had become the fourth-largest chocolate manufacturer in Britain and it was the most popular low-cost brand in the country. But the company was in decline from the mid-1920s and throughout the Second World War.

MACKINTOSH, HALIFAX

Established in 1890 by John and Violet Mackintosh in a Halifax pastry shop, the company started off making and selling Mackintosh's Celebrated Toffee. So successful was he that by 1896 John Mackintosh was styling himself 'Toffee King'. This is how he modestly heralded his entry into the US market in the 1920s:

> I am John Mackintosh, the Toffee King, Sovereign of Pleasure, Emperor of Joy. My old English candy tickles my millions of subjects ... I was crowned by the lovers of good things to eat ... I am the world's largest consumer of butter, my own herd of prize cattle graze on the Yorkshire hills. I buy sugar by the trainload. I am John Mackintosh, Toffee King of England and I rule alone.

The Halifax Rowntree Mackintosh factory, now Nestlé's, in 2010.

Chocolate-coated Toffee Deluxe was launched in 1917 followed by Mackintosh Chocolate in 1924. His son, Harold Mackintosh, later first Viscount Mackintosh of Halifax, took on the business in 1920 and developed the Methodist principles on which the firm had been founded, notably enlightened management and labour relations; in 1932 he bought the A.J. Caley confectionery company in Norwich from Unilever, which allowed Mackintosh's to expand its range of products and specialise in chocolate products such as Quality Street, launched in 1936, and Rolo, launched in 1938.

The Quality Street name comes from the play of that name by J. M. Barrie. The 'Major Quality' and 'Miss Sweetly' figures were inspired by the play's main characters and appeared on all Quality Street boxes and tins until 2000. They in turn were originally modelled by Iris and Tony Coles, the children of Sydney Coles, who created the brand's image. Mackintosh took an advertisement on the front page of the *Daily Mail* on 2 May 1936 – 'An introduction to Quality Street'. It shows Miss Sweetly tempting Major Quality with a tin of the sweets. 'Sweets to the sweet, Miss Sweetly?' asks the Major, to which she replies: 'Spare my blushes, Major Quality, feast your eyes rather on this sumptuous array of toffees and chocolates … 'tis the most momentous thing that has yet happened in the world of sweetness.' She gives him a 'toffee creme brazil', which he declares 'a veritable triumph!' Seven million Quality Street chocolates are now produced every day, the most popular being 'the Purple One'.

A scene from *Quality Street*, the J. M. Barrie play after which the chocolate was named and from which it acquired its distinctive branding.

He loves me.. he loves me not.. he loves me..

She'll get the right answer whichever she chooses... with 18 different varieties of the most adorable toffees and chocolates to choose from, Chocolate Nut Toffee Creme.. Chocolate Toffee Cup.. or perhaps Mackintosh's Dessert Toffee.. and there are still fifteen more heavenly Quality Street inspirations... What a delicious dilemma!

CHOCOLATE TOFFEE CUP
A cup of chocolate filled with almost liquid toffee.

CHOCOLATE NUT TOFFEE CREME
Inside rich milk chocolate is a nut nestling in smooth, creamy toffee.

DESSERT TOFFEE
Delicious, smooth toffee, as only Mackintosh's can make it.

Mackintosh's
'Quality Street'

No one ever says 'No' to Mackintosh's

JOHN MACKINTOSH & SONS LTD., HALIFAX

Early Quality Street advertisement showing that the seductive influence of the assortment has not diminished over the years.

Other products included Beehive Toffee from the 1920s, Creamy Rolls, whose wrapper featured a milkmaid and her cows (1920–9), Cresta (1950), Caramac (1959), Cracknel Bon-Bons, Toffo, Toffee Crisp, Golden Toffee Wafers, Munchies, the Weekend assortment in 1957, and Good News in 1960. Mackintosh was acquired by Rowntree's in 1969.

NEEDLER'S, HULL

Known principally for its confectionery, Needler's was, nevertheless, a force in the chocolate industry in the early twentieth century. At the age of eighteen Frederick Needler, a Methodist, bought a small manufacturing confectionery business for £100 and set up in Anne Street, south of Paragon Station, Hull, in 1886. In 1900 there were ten female and twenty-three male employees producing a variety of lines: thirty-eight different boiled sweets; forty types of toffees; thirty-five health sweets, fourteen pralines and fifteen different labelled sticks of rock. The company also acted as wholesalers for other firms, such as the German Quaker firm of Stollwerk, Cadbury's, Cravens of York, Taverners and Rowntree's. By 1912 the product range included 576 lines, of which seventy-four were chocolate. A new five-storey chocolate plant was built in 1916 at Bournemouth Street to cater for this. By 1920 turnover was £570,000, comprising 650 tonnes of chocolate and 1,500 tonnes of sweets, with a range now including Christmas boxes and Easter eggs. There were 1,700 employees, mainly female. In 1929 the catalogue featured twelve different assortment boxes and numerous chocolate bars. The boxes gloried in such names as Wilberforce, Minaret, Lido, Eldora, Carlton and Crown Derby. Kreema milk chocolate was advertised as being 'Creamy! Velvety! Delicious!'

A Fred Needler delivery van in Spring Bank, Hull, in the 1930s.

MELTIS, BEDFORD

Meltis was set up by Peek Frean & Co. in 1913 to produce peppermints, glacé fruits and the chocolate coverings for their biscuits; Meltis soon expanded to manufacture chocolate in its own right. In 1931 Meltis began to make chocolate for Suchard, an alliance which lasted into the 1980s, producing a wide range of products including prestige chocolate selections in elaborate packaging. In 1933 the Duchess of York range of assorted chocolates was launched and the top of the range 4-lb deluxe box of Assorted Superfine Chocolates entered the market at 17s 6d.

A Meltis box of assorted chocolates.

Meltis continued to develop new products, and in the 1950s chocolate liqueurs were introduced, becoming a leading product line up to the 1970s. In 1961 a new chocolate plant was installed to produce 100 tonnes of liquid chocolate per week. Meltis was now the largest producer of Turkish Delight and crystallised fruit in Britain, and the second-largest producer of liqueurs. In 1975 Interfood, the owners of Suchard, took over Tobler Meltis. Jacobs purchased Interfood in 1982 and Jacob Suchard was formed. The company went into receivership in 1996.

GREEN & BLACK'S, LONDON

Craig Sams and Josphine Fairley founded Green & Black's in 1991 as an organic, Fairtrade company, producing dark chocolate bars with a high cocoa content. The name was inspired by traditional brand-names but plays on its modern ethics, the 'green' representing the organic principles of its production and the 'black' the dark chocolate typically produced by the brand, which also produces ice cream, biscuits and hot chocolate. The company was purchased by Cadbury's in 2005, and was part of the sale to Kraft in 2010, but continues to operate on its own terms.

DIVINE CHOCOLATE LTD, LONDON

Originally known as the Day Chocolate Company, this ethical manufacturer of Fairtrade chocolate products was established in the United Kingdom in 1998 as a partnership between the Kuapa Kokoo cocoa growers' collective in Ghana and the alternative trading organisation Twin Trading; other supporters included The Body Shop, Christian Aid and Comic Relief. The farmers own 45 per cent of the company on a profit-sharing basis. Its first product, launched in 1998, was Divine milk chocolate. Divine white chocolate, flavoured milk chocolate, dark chocolate and drinking chocolate have since followed.

FOREIGN CHOCOLATE COMPANIES IN BRITAIN

MARS, USA

Frank C. Mars launched the Mar-O-Bar in 1922 with the Minneapolis-based Mar-O-Bar Company; initially the Mar-O-Bar was not a great success, mainly on account of its fragility. Milky Way followed in 1923 – an immediate hit promoted as 'chocolate malted milk in a candy bar'. In 1929 the company moved to Chicago and Frank's son, Forrest E. Mars Senior, joined the company. The original Snickers bar was launched in 1930. Forrest arrived in England in 1932 with £5,000 and set up Mars Ltd in a rented factory in Slough with twelve staff; he launched the Mars Bar as a sweeter version of the US Milky Way (which itself is quite different from the European market Milky Way). The US variety of Mars Bar is also quite different from its European counterpart in that it is like a sweeter version of our Milky Way. Initially the bars were coated in chocolate supplied by Cadbury ('Why ever did we do that?', Sir Adrian Cadbury wryly asked) and they were such a success that staff increased from twelve to over a hundred within a year. Mars Ltd, an incredibly secretive company, demonstrated many of the philanthropic industrial welfare initiatives of the indigenous Quaker companies: they included a pension plan, an in-house doctor, a cafeteria and a company newsletter. Mars paid well and in return demanded long hours and the highest quality in their products. Today, over two million Mars Bars are produced every day in Britain alone.

Maltesers appeared in 1935 and Mars Bars were supplied in 1940 for the troops and for prisoners of war in Germany. In 1960 the phrase 'A Mars a day helps you work, rest and play' was heard for the first time. That same year Galaxy was launched in competition to Dairy Milk with Britain's biggest ever television advertising campaign. In 1982 M&Ms were the first sweets to be taken into outer space when the crew of the first space shuttle included them in their food packs, and 3 million Mars Bars were taken with the task force to the Falklands. M&Ms (named after the company's founders) had been launched in the United States in 1941 as a cheaper alternative to Smarties. Forrest Mars Senior got the idea when he saw soldiers in the Spanish Civil War eating chocolate pellets with a hard shell of tempered chocolate

Opposite:
A 1910 Boisellier showcard emphasising the romantic nature of its chocolates.

Above: Dutch company Van Houten's advertisement promoting quality and value for money.

Above right: Mars Bar fulfilling the 'play' aspect of its famous three-part slogan.

Quality and the seductive nature of Nestlé's chocolate are shown in this advertisement.

surrounding the inside, preventing the candies from melting. A black 'M' first appeared on each sweet in 1950, later changed to white in 1954. The two-bar Bounty was launched in 1951, Treets in 1955, Galaxy in 1960, Topic in 1962 and, in 1967, Twix, Revels and Marathon, later re-branded as Snickers.

NESTLÉ, SWITZERLAND

Henri Nestlé was born in Frankfurt in 1814; in 1875, thirty-two years after moving to Vevey on Lake Geneva in 1843, the chemist started making *farine lactée*, a baby food (*Kindermehl*) made from Alpine milk in powder form and ground cereal. As we have seen, Henri Nestlé with Daniel Peter and Jean-Jacques Kohler, his chocolate manufacturing neighbours, then went on to develop the first real milk chocolate when the businessmen combined their products to produce Chocolat au Lait Gala Peter – 'The Original Milk Chocolate' – in 1874. Henri opened a sales office in London in 1883 for the Farine Lactée Henri Nestlé Company and in 1901 its first British factory began production. Nestlé merged with the Anglo-Swiss Condensed Milk Company in 1905 to form the Nestlé and Anglo-Swiss Milk Company. Sales were boosted by Nestlé's extensive use of the new vending machines, which were springing up everywhere and which, in this case, dispensed 1d chocolate bars. In 1904 they made an agreement with Kohler and Cailler to import their chocolate products and thus strengthened their position in the UK market. In 1913 chocolate production began at Hayes. The white chocolate Milky Bar was launched in 1937 and soon gained a reputation for being good for children because it contained only cocoa butter, sugar and milk; it is made entirely from natural ingredients without artificial colours or flavours. Nearly half a pint of milk is poured into every 100g of chocolate.

In 1988 Nestlé acquired Rowntree Mackintosh and in 2010 Nestlé celebrated the seventy-fifth anniversary of KitKat. The Nestlé UK website

Le
Bébé
NESTLÉ
fait
l'admiration
de tous

The famous Nestlé baby winning all-round admiration in French-speaking markets.

gives us the following amazing statistics: over 1 billion KitKats are eaten in the United Kingdom every year, equal to 564 fingers every second; 17.6 billion fingers are eaten across the world every year; and the largest single retail outlet for KitKat is Dubai Duty Free, which sells over 1 tonne per day. Three million KitKats are made every day in York.

TOBLERONE, SWITZERLAND

In 1868 Jean Tobler ran a confectionery shop called Confiserie Speciale in Bern, Switzerland, producing chocolate sweets from products supplied by other manufacturers. By 1899 Tobler's chocolates were so successful that Tobler set up his own factory with his sons: the Fabrique de Chocolat Berne, Tobler & Cie. In 1900 Theodor Tobler took over the business and exports to countries including Britain began that year. In 1908 with his cousin Emil Baumann he invented the unique milk chocolate bar that is Toblerone. A new factory was built in 1985, with every Toblerone produced there. Dark Toblerone was launched in 1969 with White Toblerone following in 1973.

Below: An early Toblerone advertisement aimed at 'jolly and friendly people' at 'the jolliest and most successful picnics', as well as at extreme sportsmen and women.

Below right: more seduction, this time from Toblerone – note the man's hand.

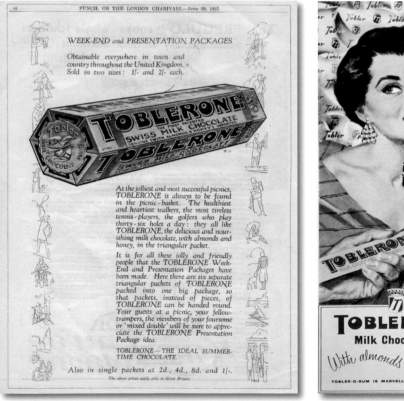

The 1990s saw rapid product expansion with Minis in 1995, Blue in 1996 (the first filled Toblerone) and Praline in 1997. In 2007 Toblerone Fruit & Nut entered the market. Other brands include Honeycomb Crisp and Tobelles – Toblerone thins in a yellow triangular box.

The name 'Toblerone' is derived from the chocolatier's family name 'Tobler' and '*torrone*', the Italian for nougat. It is commonly believed that Theodor Tobler fashioned the unique shape of his chocolate on the mountain scenery of Switzerland, and on the Matterhorn in particular. But the truth is much more exotic: according to Theodor's sons, the bar was inspired by the red and cream-frilled line of dancers at the Folies Bergères in Paris, who formed a shapely pyramid at the finale of each show.

Prudently, Theodor Tobler and Tobler AG applied for a patent in 1909 in Bern to cover the manufacture and shape of the bar and Toblerone thus became the first patented milk chocolate bar. The official who gave the authorising signature was one Albert Einstein, who was working in the Patent Office at the time. A picture of a bear – the civic symbol of Bern – lurks in the Matterhorn mountain image on the packaging. In 2000, after cigarettes, the biggest selling line in airport duty-free shops was Toblerone.

In 1970 Toblerone merged with Suchard to become Interfood and then with Jacobs in 1982 to create Jacobs Suchard. Kraft acquired Jacobs Suchard in 1990.

Above left:
This Toblerone advertisement, complete with press review, plays on the brand's association with the high arts.

Above right:
A Chocolat Tobler Ltd trade calling card sent in August 1930 by traveller H. Chadwick to a customer in Colwyn Bay requesting an appointment.

AFTER THE SECOND WORLD WAR

A FTER the Second World War the privations suffered by the chocolate companies were to continue until 1953, when rationing was finally ended. To make matters worse, cocoa disease wiped out 16 per cent of the world's cocoa supply in 1948, thus pushing up the price to £237 per tonne – six times the pre-war price. It was a period of consolidation for all the companies.

Cadbury, in the face of all this austerity, launched Fudge in 1949. To meet the surge in demand for confectionery after 1953 more factory space was needed at Cadbury. The move from selling biscuits loose in tins to packets, brought about by the development of self-service shops, meant that for Cadbury a new factory was needed; this opened on 17 September 1954 at Moreton on the Wirral to turn out 3 million chocolate biscuits every day; Somerdale was extended in 1958 to cater for Picnic. Cadbury's Buttons came

The wrecked Caley factory in Norwich after the 1942 'Baedeker' raid.

70

in 1960 followed by Bar Six to compete with KitKat. The launch of Aztec in 1967 was the most significant event of the post-war period. Aimed squarely at the Mars Bar market, it benefited from a merchandising campaign that was included in store displays in over 100,000 shops and a television advertising campaign filmed on the steps of the Aztec temples in Teotihuacan, no less. The predicament of Fry and Cadbury representatives calling on shops and fighting each other for display space was ended in 1967 when the two companies formed a full merger.

In 1969 Cadbury joined up with Schweppes – a firm founded in Geneva in 1783 by Jean Jacob Schweppe, who had perfected a method of carbonating water. This was despite Cadbury's reservations about Schweppes' association with alcohol (its drinks were used as mixers) and the impact this would have on the Quakers' intolerance to alcohol – one of the original *raisons d'êtres* for cocoa manufacture and promotion in the previous century.

Curly Wurly, Double Decker, Star Bar and Caramel were next to come off the production lines. In 1978 Chunky Dairy Milk was developed to counter Rowntree's highly successful Yorkie. In 1981 Wispa (codename P46) was successfully developed as a competitor to Aero, tactically withdrawn and then relaunched in 1983, backed by Cadbury's biggest ever campaign. The size of the bubbles are controlled to within 0.2–0.3mm and the specially

Austere Cadbury ration lines were produced under difficult conditions and supplied to the services during the Second World War.

Rowntree's workers training for a gas attack.

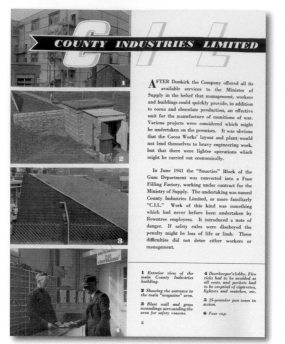

Various scenes from County Industries, the munitions company formed at Rowntree's, taken from *The Cocoa Works in War-time*: (1) the converted Smarties block; (2) main magazine area; (3) blast wall; (4) doorkeeper – 'contraband' was a euphemism for fire risk materials such as cigarettes and matches.

designed £12 million plant, constructed in great secrecy produced 1,680 bars per minute. In 1988 Cadbury purchased first the Lion Confectionery Company of Cleckheaton (famous for Midget Gems) and then Trebor Bassett, which led to the development of Cadbury's Mini Creme Egg – 700 million of which are made each year.

In York at Rowntree's, Munchies were reintroduced; the Fawdon factory, Newcastle, opened in 1958 and in 1959 Caramac was launched. Nux was brought to market in 1959 but lost the battle against Fry's Picnic. Peppermint and orange Aeros came in 1959 and 1960 respectively. 1962 saw the launch of After Eight with its sophisticated dinner party market, followed by Toffee Crisp a year later. Motoring Bar was renamed Fruit and Nut in 1963 but could not compete with its namesake down at Cadbury and was killed off in 1965. In 1967 Golden Cup was introduced and Matchmakers arrived in 1968.

Having acquired Chocolat Menier in 1969, Rowntree then bought Mackintosh, so bringing such household names as Rolo, Toffee Crisp, Toffo, Weekend and Quality Street to the fold. Aimed unusually more at the male than the traditional female market, Yorkie was launched in 1976 to compete with Cadbury's Dairy Milk and to meet the demand for a chunkier alternative to the much thinner Dairy Milk bars. Yorkie was soon a major success, with sales of 13,000 tonnes by 1978.

KitKat continued to dominate, however. A corporate advertisement in 1987 asserts that enough KitKats are produced every hour to reach to the top of the Empire State Building four times over, and 30 million KitKats are sold in one hundred countries every week. March 2008 saw the arrival of Kit Kat Senses with one of the biggest confectionery launches ever aimed at the female market. In 1988 Rowntree Mackintosh was the world's fourth largest confectionery manufacturer after Hershey, Mars and Cadbury; turnover was £1.4 billion in twenty-five subsidiaries with 33,000 employees. A takeover bid by Jacobs Suchard in 1988 failed (Suchard had already acquired Côte d'Or and Van Houten) but that same year Rowntree Mackintosh was acquired by Nestlé, despite unsuccessful attempts by Cadbury to keep Rowntree British by appealing to the Department of Trade and Industry to relax competition rules and allow them to acquire Rowntree Mackintosh.

A replica Terry's chocolate shop was opened in the Castle Museum in York in the 1950s. In 1980 the elegant Terry's restaurant in St Helen's Square closed after 150 years. When the factory closed in 2005, over four hundred objects, including photographs, packaging, catalogues and chocolates, were donated to the Castle Museum. In the 1990s annual sales of All Gold were 7 million boxes; All Gold revenue was £11 million in 1981, doubling by 1990. At its zenith Terry was selling 23,000 tons of chocolate, 56 million Chocolate Oranges, and Easter eggs weighing 650 tons. Moments were launched in 1991 with a new £7 million pound moulding plant. In 1987 confectionery sales in the United Kingdom were just over £3 billion; by comparison bread was £1.7 billion and milk was £1.6 billion.

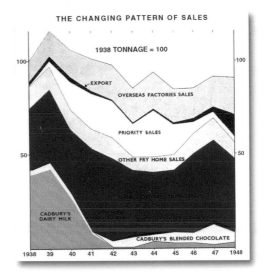

THE CHANGING PATTERN OF SALES

1938 TONNAGE = 100

EXPORT

OVERSEAS FACTORIES SALES

PRIORITY SALES

OTHER FRY HOME SALES

CADBURY'S DAIRY MILK

CADBURY'S BLENDED CHOCOLATE

Cadbury sales before, during and after the war (1938–48) clearly showing the depressing effect.

Mr. N. G. Sparkes, the Gum Department Manager, was appointed to take charge of the new venture.

"Magazines" for the storage of explosives had to be constructed adjacent to the cricket field. The process consisted of filling fuses with explosive powder and detonators. The fuses were required in vast quantities, particularly for fusing 25-pounder shells.

Fuses such as these made at County Industries Limited, the munitions company formed at Rowntree to make fuses, were used mainly in 25-pounder shells for artillery. The aptly named Mr N. G. Sparkes, Gum Department Manager, was in charge.

Fortune
makes the heart
grow fonder

MARKETING

W E HAVE SEEN how from earliest days chocolate has been closely associated with aphrodisiacs, romance and the wooing of women. This association has been endlessly exploited by the chocolate companies and their advertising agents in the marketing of chocolate products. (Early market research found that 60 per cent of all chocolate boxes were bought by men as gifts for women.) It extends from early advertisements and posters through television and, today, corporate and product websites. You only have to think of the mildly sexual Flake television advertisements of the 1970s, 'The lady loves Milk Tray', the coy girl on the Caley's Monarch Assortment, and 'Caley's Fortune makes the heart grow fonder' to get the picture.

Black Magic, which combines the occult with the erotic, captured the mood in its 1939 trade catalogue:

> Caught me under the misletoe! I was just about to give the wretch a piece of my mind when he whipped out a box of Black Magic. So what could I do? Those chocs would soften the hardest heart.

Perhaps their most explicit advertising copy, though, was this from 1934:

> We silly creatures are always so thrilled when a man thinks us worth the very best. Imagine it, a big box of these new Black Magic chocolates on my dressing table. My dear, each choc's an orgy!

The distinctive black box endured more or less for sixty years until 2007; they were, nevertheless, relaunched in 2009 by popular demand.

After Eight sent a similar message:

> According to Cynthia, the Squeeze is what happens in taxis with an admirer, and the Freeze is when he forgets to buy her After Eight.

Opposite:
This hair-raising
July 1953 *Punch*
advertisement
shows clearly that
Caley's chocolate
'makes the heart
grow fonder'.

The After Eight display (also showing stills from the television advertisements) in Joe Dickinson's collection in York. After Eight was aimed squarely at the upwardly mobile, aspirational, sophisticated dinner party market, the perfect compliment to posh coffee, Bailey's and Trivial Pursuit.

The introduction of wrappers, of course, facilitated branding; until the end of the nineteenth century chocolates were sold loose in wooden boxes. One of the earliest examples of successful wrapper branding was Fry's Five Boys, launched in 1886 for Fry's Milk Chocolate, showing a range of emotions excited by eating Fry's chocolate: 'Desperation, Pacification, Expectation, Acclamation and … the Realization that it's Fry's'. A matching poster appeared in 1905 telling us: 'The "Five Girls" want Fry's "Five Boys" Milk Chocolate and will have no other.'

At the same time advertisements, posters and show cards demonstrated another universal and enduring theme – that chocolate is quite simply exceedingly nice to eat. A 1927 Cadbury poster tells us that their chocolate has 'tastes that thrill', and Terry's took no prisoners when they launched their Theobroma assortment –with the added slogan 'Wait until she sees inside'.

Chocolate boxes too, for assortments, offered another vehicle for branding and eye-catching illustration. From 1862 Fry's and Cadbury's were selling chocolates in boxes, particularly at Easter and Christmas; in 1882 Rowntree's had no fewer than 150 different boxes on offer. Sentimentality was the order of the day in artwork and apart from its primary, immediate use the chocolate box was often a long-term repository for odds and ends, photographs, postcards and other keepsakes — long fuse, slow drip advertising. Cadbury's indeed produced some very lavish boxes plush-lined with silk and satin and designed to hold jewellery, handkerchiefs or gloves long after the chocolates were eaten.

Tins followed and these too produced vivid and colourful designs with immediate and long-term functions, as many a cupboard and loft will attest.

The very product names were put to work at selling: Mackintosh's Egg & Cream Toffee Deluxe, for example, was an early version of us getting precisely what it says on the tin. In the 1990s Terry's redesigned their All Gold and Moonlight boxes to target the fifteen to twenty-four-year-old market, which made up 24 per cent of sales: the former were shaped into ingots, the latter into dinner-jacket shaped boxes with Art Nouveau illustrations.

If the romantic qualities of chocolate were aimed mostly at the middle classes, then the nutritional and energy characteristics were somewhat less class-bound. Alleged health benefits were a factor in the expansion of sales of milk chocolate in the early twentieth century, aided by claims of high nutritional values afforded by rich, pure milk content. This chimed with the traditional claims surrounding so-called medicinal confectionery: lozenges, voice jujubes and barley sugar, for example, all claimed medical benefits, as indeed did Mackintosh's toffee – good for sore throats. Betty's Tea Rooms,

The interior of Terry's restaurant in the 1930s. The menu for the day comprised anchovy toast, mock turtle soup, turbot aurora, curried chicken and rice, vegetables and fruit salad – all for 4 shillings.

FRY'S MILK CHOCOLATE

DESPERATION. PACIFICATION. EXPECTATION. ACCLAMATION. REALIZATION.
'IT'S FRYS'

J.S. FRY & SONS LTD BRISTOL & LONDON.

Fry's famous Five Boys advertisement extolling the satisfying, calming influence of chocolate – every mother's dream and passport to a quieter life, it seems.

Opposite: Coy lady promoting Caley chocolates in the late 1920s.

who produced their own chocolate for sale in their York and Harrogate cafés, told us that eating chocolate actually does lead to weight loss. Posters and advertisements were populated with healthy, pink-cheeked children.

Cadbury's Dairy Milk Chocolate (or CDM) was 'rich in cream'. 'Overflowing with goodness' was trotted out by both Mackintosh and Nestlé while Pascall's Ambrosia Devonshire Chocolate was 'the glory of Devon in a packet'. Fry's famous churn-shaped show card from 1925 announced that their milk chocolate contained 'full cream milk from west of England farms'. In 1955 Mars was still telling us that not only was a Mars Bar good for your work–life balance but also that it 'feeds you goodness 3 good ways: milk, chocolate, glucose'.

The *British Medical Journal* of 26 December 1891 endorsed Bovril Chocolate (Bovril Caramels containing 10 per cent Bovril), and Oxo Chocolate was manufactured on a similar basis – 'a stand-by between meals'. Bovril's claim was that it contained '300 per cent more actual nourishment than any other chocolate extant'.

Below: Cadbury chocolate assortment box illustrations from 1869–70, designed by Richard Cadbury and typical of the prevailing fashion for Victorian sentimentality. The little girl nursing her cat (pictured top centre) is one of his daughters.

THE COMING OF THE FANCY BOX.

The idea that chocolate boxes should bear pictures instead of printed labels was conceived by Richard Cadbury in 1868. His artistic talent was always invaluable to the business, and it was he who designed the first fancy boxes introduced, as well as numerous box-labels and advertisements. The picture box readily caught the public fancy, and did much to popularise the firm's lines generally. The designs shown are reproduced as a record of his talent as they appear on a page in the "Cadbury Family Book."

Right:
Fry's Crunchie advertisement with its slogan and visual suggestion that a girl biting into a Crunchie attracts a boy.

Below: An early Cadbury's Dairy Milk advertisement promoting the fresh milk content of the bar. The Knighton churn tower (bottom right) cleaned churns using blasts of high-powered steam, raised them to the top to dry and then lowered them, ready to be returned to the dairy farms.

It was particularly suitable for children and the sick, as well as being good for sportsmen and travellers: 'a food by the way'; 'a perfect food in itself'. Oxo also marketed Oxo Toffee (containing fluid beef and fresh cream milk) as did Boots – Vitamalt Toffee – while Horlicks produced a malted milk toffee. Terry's Snack was ideal for walkers as it contained raisins and 'nutritive' cereals. Mars initially launched Maltesers as low fat 'energy balls'.

British companies were not immune from nostalgic and, by today's standards, racist advertising, harking back to the days of slavery and ongoing or recently lapsed colonialism. German chocolates were branded *Negrokusse* and *Mohrenkopfe* and Sarotti's symbol of the Sarotti Moor was depicted with racially exaggerated features similar to the now banished golliwog. A Fry's advertisement from the turn of the century has a crowd of negroes

marvelling at a cargo of Fry's cocoa washed up on their island: 'a new discovery' – somewhat patronising if one recalls the tens of thousands of slaves employed in the cocoa industry not so many years before.

The consumption of chocolate was often associated with everyday life: Caley's Marching Chocolate was aimed at the military; Rowntree's Motoring Chocolate, from 1928, was just as essential as petrol and aimed at the glove box ('You can't go without it!'); Cadbury's Holiday Chocolate and Excursion Chocolate were targeted at the increasing number of motorists, day trippers and holiday makers, as were Payne's Poppets: 'Stop at the shop that has Poppets' and 'add that touch of surprise that makes the holiday … make this a real

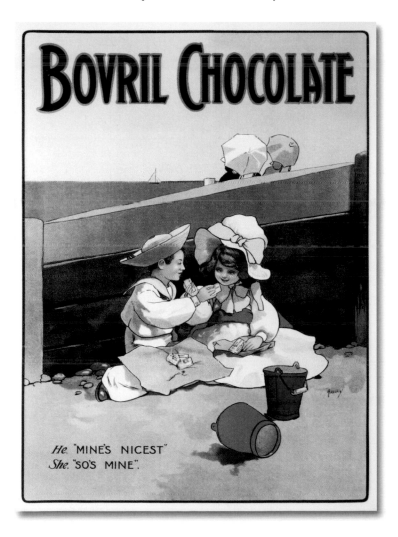

If Bovril was to be believed in this 1902 poster by John Hassall, the bonding qualities involved in sharing chocolate begin at an early age. Bovril boasted that their chocolate contained 300 per cent more nourishment than any other chocolate.

Poppet of a holiday.' Chocolate cigars and cigarettes were popular and packaged to look like the real thing, with Dunn's, Fry's and Rowntree's all involved.

Rowntree's indulged in some advertising stunts in the late 1890s: organised by Joseph Rowntree's nephew Arnold. One of those new-fangled motor cars toured the country with a giant Elect Cocoa tin on the back, and during the 1897 Oxford and Cambridge boat race a barge covered in Elect posters crossed the Thames. In 1976 Terry's launched their All Gold hot-air balloon, the only gold balloon in the world at that time.

Less dramatically, the need to win repeat business was developed through the use of coupons, prizes and collecting cards on all manner of subjects by

A colourful advertisement for a colourful product; by the standards of the day (the 1950s) this was not inappropriate.

all the main British companies and by Nestlé. Christmas and Easter have always been peak times: seasonal catalogues offering their special ranges were produced from the 1920s. Selection boxes were aggressively promoted with games and puzzles on the boxes.

Easter eggs were first produced in the 1870s by Fry's and Cadbury's, and sweets were soon filling them; free gifts became popular in the 1930s with toys such as quacking ducks inside and packaging inspired by light-bulb carton designers.

Innovative, and by today's standards decidedly odd, receptacles were used as containers for chocolates: Rowntree's had a chrome teapot; Nestlé a Royal Winton teapot; Fry's a brass coal scuttle or a pickle jar; and Needler's the Knitcraft case – 'a useful and attractive container for your work, wool, needles &c'.

By the beginning of the Second World War the UK market alone was huge and the stakes were high – there were over 300,000 shops selling sweets and chocolates supplied by around 350 confectionery and chocolate producers. Advertising hoardings, shop windows, show cards and point of sale as well as newspaper and magazine advertisements were all crucial to the promotion of a seemingly endless stream of new products. In the 1950s Cadbury had sixty permanent display men responsible for window displays and point of sale the length and breadth of the country, backed up by two hundred representatives.

Postcards – often featuring the images from the show cards – were extremely popular and collected from the earliest days right up to modern times, and they are still much sought after.

The famous Rowntree's Elect Cocoa barge passing under Hungerford Bridge on the River Thames during the 1899 Boat Race. The name 'Elect' was chosen because of its association with efficaciousness.

Cadbury was quick to recognise the value of good public relations. They set up a Visitors' Department in 1902 and were receiving 150,000 people a day up to 1939 – many of them on organised bus or rail excursions. A 2-mile tour of the factory and of Bournville awaited them, with refreshments and a film. This all had to stop for the war and then again in 1970, when health and safety regulations demanded compliance with the same rigorous hygiene procedures for visitors as for production line workers. But public demand helped the establishment of the £6 million Cadbury World in 1990, with 420,000 visitors going through the doors soon after opening. Research had shown that visitors were more likely to buy Cadbury products up to twenty years after their visit.

It is no surprise that confectionery companies were among the first advertisers on commercial television on its launch in 1955. By 1958, 60 per cent of the chocolate advertising budget went on television commercials. Some of the more memorable confectionery slogans include 'Murray Mints, the too-good-to-hurry-mints' and 'Don't forget the Fruit Gums, Mum.' Polar cool Polos were 'the mint with the hole', and in 1957 we were invited to 'have a break … have a KitKat'. The Milky Bar Kid first rode into town in 1961 and the Bond-like Milk Tray hero overcame almost insurmountable odds most nights from 1968 to get that box to his intended – 'all because the lady loves Milk Tray'. (He made his last surreptitious delivery in 2003 to the strains of Cliff Adams's *Night Rider*, as usual.) Milky Way was known as 'the

A Terry's television advertisement for All Gold – the 'wooing of women' message becoming increasingly explicit.

sweet you can eat between meals', and 'a finger of Fudge is just enough to give your kids a treat'. Cadbury's Flake proved that 'only the crumbliest, flakiest chocolate tastes like chocolate never tasted before', and Terry's Chocolate Orange became famous for its striking marketing. Slogans included: 'When you whack a Terry's Chocolate Orange, good things happen'; 'Tap it and unwrap it'; 'It's not Terry's, it's mine', and 'Don't tap it ... whack it'. Recent television advertising campaigns carry the slogan 'Smash it to pieces, love it to bits'.

In 1988 the Cadbury brand – as opposed to individual lines – was relaunched, mainly through television advertising and with the slogan: 'Cadbury's. The Chocolate. The Taste.' Cadbury's Dairy Milk was the vehicle, focusing on the four instantly recognisable pillars of brand Cadbury: the colour purple, a swirl of chocolate, a glass and a half, and the Cadbury signature. The seductive refrain of the popular song 'Show Me Heaven' could be heard in the background.

Perhaps the most significant move in modern television advertising occurred in 1996 when Cadbury became sponsors of *Coronation Street* – Britain's longest-running soap opera, now more than fifty years old. The initial cost was £10 million for one year but this ensured that the Cadbury name and associated icons were on our screens at the beginning and end of each episode and at every commercial break.

Stills from the Fry's Turkish Delight television advertisements, full of eastern promise and more exoticism and mild eroticism.

"Scenes from the new TV commercials for Fry's Turkish Delight in the 1980's."

Fry's Turkish Delight.   Full of eastern promise

Changes in the retail landscape obviously influenced chocolate marketing. Self-service grocers and supermarkets gradually replaced the traditional grocers and confectioner-tobacconist-newsagent: their eye-catching window displays gave way to display units and point of sale. A move towards the use of wholesalers as opposed to the company traveller or representative had a similar impact on how chocolate was displayed in shops: merchandising had arrived and impulse buying – pioneered by Mars – was the way forward.

Retail price maintenance was lifted on confectionery in the early 1960s allowing cut-price chocolates, multi-packs and mini-packs containing 'fun-size' bars. The effect of this is exemplified by KitKat: 20 per cent of all sales were in multi-packs by 1970. Voucher schemes, personalities hosting lavish prize competitions, the famous philanthropic CDM award for Cadbury's Dairy Milk all added to the marketing mix at one time or another. Cadbury's *CocoCub News* was an enormously successful children's magazine which had 300,000 readers at its peak and was centred on the activities of a character named Jonathan. It grew out of an equally successful campaign in 1936 featuring a special tin of cocoa targeted at children and containing highly collectible free miniature animals such as Nutty Squirrel, Dan Crow and Monty Monkey.

Quality artists were often employed to great effect: Caley, Bovril Chocolate and Fry used John Hassall – most famous for his *The Jolly Fisherman* poster created in 1908 for the Great Northern Railway; Fry's commissioned Tom Browne, one of the best of the British comic postcard artists at the beginning of the twentieth century, and Chas Pears, a prolific

The ground-breaking Cadbury *Coronation Street* television advertisement.

poster artist for the London Underground and an official war artist in both world wars. Alfred Leete drew Rowntree's Mr York in 1928; before that he had produced 'Your Country Needs You' in 1914 – probably the best-known war poster of all time. Mackintosh used Jean d'Ylen, celebrated French poster artist, for their Toffee de Luxe in 1929, as well as Heath Robinson, cartoonist and illustrator, best known for his drawings of crazy machines, and Mabel Lucie Atwell, book and magazine illustrator, for *Toffee Town*, as used in national newspaper advertisements. Raymond Peynet, creator of the famous 'Les Amoureux', worked on Dairy Box and Sir Alfred Mullins, celebrated painter of horses, drew Caley's famous Marquee and Lady posters. G. M. Elwood designed some of their chocolate boxes around 1922. Richard Cadbury, an accomplished artist in his own right, worked on some of his own chocolate boxes. Cadbury's used Arthur Rackham's work on its chocolate boxes and a team of top comic illustrators for its popular *CocoCub News* in 1935. CocoCubs also featured comic strips in the national press, drawn by top artists of the day.

The cover from an early *CocoCub News*. CocoCub Club was launched in 1936 and by 1938 had 300,000 members; the Second World War killed it off.

The 1935 Christmas card does not open out. The back and front are separated by a central wheel that rotates to reveal some of the cubs in a window in the shape of a Christmas tree.

Activity CocoCub Christmas card courtesy of Jonathan and Mr Pie Porker.

THE TWENTY-FIRST CENTURY

THE TWENTY-FIRST CENTURY has already seen significant changes in the chocolate industry in Britain, not least Kraft's £11.5bn takeover of Cadbury in 2010 to add to its earlier acquisitions of Terry's and Toblerone. Fairtrade and the Internet have undoubtedly underpinned the biggest industry-wide developments.

According to figures released by *UK Confectionery Review*, Cadbury Trebor Bassett and others, each person eats on average about two hundred bars of chocolate every year. We spend nearly £4 billion on chocolate around 70 per cent of the total UK confectionery market (chocolate and sweets). More than 90 per cent of the UK population buys confectionery, with each buyer spending an average of 30p a day. Nearly two-thirds of all confectionery is purchased by women, but they eat just over a half of what they buy themselves; men purchase just under a third of all confectionery and generally eat the majority of what they buy; children eat 38 per cent of all confectionery, but buy only 20 per cent of what they eat themselves. A recent report showed that people over fifty-five eat £700 worth of chocolate every year, 21 per cent of the total chocolate and confectionery sold in Britain.

In 2010 the biggest cacao producers were the Ivory Coast (33 per cent), Ghana (21 per cent) and Indonesia (15 per cent). Brazil (4 per cent) saw its output virtually wiped out by a fungal disease, witches' broom, in 1989, when it had been the world's second largest producer. The biggest consumers in 2010 were the United States (17.8 per cent), the Netherlands (14.1 per cent), the Far East (12.2 per cent), Germany, France and Brazil (all between 6 and 7 per cent) and the United Kingdom at 3.7 per cent. Total consumption was 3.5 million tonnes. The price of cacao doubled from US$1,504 per tonne in 2005 to $3,071 in 2010.

On the continuing issue of the alleged health benefits of chocolate the European Commission Food Safety Authority ruled in 2010 that there was still insufficient consistent scientific evidence to support studies which suggest that consumption of certain types of chocolate can lower blood pressure, reduce the risk of heart attack, prevent wrinkles or increase cognitive skills. However, a

Opposite:
Modern wrappers
for a modern
world.

Rowntree's page from Nestlé's website in 2011.

2010 study of 19,357 patients (EPIC Study 1994–2006), led by Brian Buijsse of the German Institute of Human Nutrition in Nuthetal and reported in the *British Heart Journal*, provided reliable evidence that chocolate does appear to offer some protection against hypertension and stroke: work is still in progress.

In 2010 Cadbury made plans to drop the eighty-year-old 'glass and a half' slogan from Dairy Milk wrappers in response to European Union rules that all weights and measures must be in metric. The somewhat less pithy 'the equivalent of 426ml of fresh liquid milk in every 227g of milk chocolate' will probably not be used as a replacement, although the memorable image of the glass and a half of milk will live on.

On 3 April 2007, Thorntons set up what is thought to be the world's first edible advertising hoarding. The 14.5-foot by 9.5-foot and 860lb sign was set up outside their Covent Garden shop, and was eaten by passers-by within three hours; it included ten chocolate bunnies, seventy-two giant chocolate eggs and 128 chocolate panels.

The 2009 relaunch of Wispa was celebrated by the production of a bar covered in edible gold leaf and costing £961.48.

In marketing, the biggest development has undoubtedly been the emergence of the corporate website where companies across the whole range of manufacturers – from Cadbury and Nestlé to Caley and Tunnock's – imaginatively and dynamically display all aspects of their manufacturing processes, heritage, recipes and ethical credentials. Individual products have their own sites giving nutritional information and a wealth of other detail; on-line stores tempt us with attractively presented brands easily and conveniently obtainable without leaving the house.

Josephine Fairley and Maya Gold neatly bring us full circle, back to the Maya Indians and the origins of the cocoa and chocolate industries. Her fairness and the wider work of the Fairtrade Foundation remind us also of the philanthropy we associate with chocolate manufacture through the famous English Quaker companies and others in the United States and in continental Europe.

With financial backing from Mars, the genetic code of the cocoa tree was finally sequenced in 2010, a major breakthrough which could lead to the tripling of the global yield and improve the lives of the millions of largely subsistence farmers dependent on the crop. Currently growers receive 3.5 per cent of the value of a bar of chocolate sold, compared to 16 per cent in 1990. Over the same period the manufacturers' cut has risen from 56 to 70 per cent.

To help address this crisis, Fairtrade has emerged as a powerful force, compelling manufacturers to pay growers a fairer price for their raw materials. The Fairtrade Foundation was originally founded by Oxfam and others and the concept was extended into the world of chocolate in 1994 by Josephine Fairley, who insisted that the chocolate she used in her new Green & Black's organic chocolate company was made from pesticide-free cacao beans. The result was Maya Gold, which not only was pesticide-free but also was produced with a fair price paid to the Kekchi Maya farmers. It was the Britain's first chocolate product to receive Fairtrade certification.

The Rowntree Inca wrapper design maintains the link with chocolate's Mesoamerican origins.

In 2009 Cadbury's Dairy Milk was Fairtrade certified, thereby tripling the amount of Fairtrade cocoa sourced from Ghana to about 15,000 tonnes a year. The total annual cocoa production of Ghana is more than 600,000 tonnes. Under Fairtrade, Cadbury pays a guaranteed minimum price, even if the open market price falls below it, for Ghanaian cocoa. The move is part of the Cadbury Cocoa Partnership, a £45 million initiative over ten years, which will help cocoa farmers throughout the developing world.

January 2010 saw the first Fairtrade-certified KitKat four-finger bars arrive on shop shelves to the benefit of thousands of farmers in Ivory Coast. As well as the Fairtrade price (or market price if higher) for the cocoa, farmers' organisations receive additional Fairtrade premium payments (currently US$150 per tonne) which are used for business or social development projects. The country produces over 30 per cent of the world's cocoa and one in four people directly or indirectly depend on cocoa farming.

Above: Modern wrapper design for Time Out.

Middle and right: Nestlé's KitKat and Cadbury's Dairy Milk packaging, both bearing the distinctive Fairtrade certified logo.

A 2010 advertisement for Ferrero, a brand that continues to be sold using luxury credentials.

FURTHER READING

Baren, M. *How It All Began in Yorkshire*. Dalesman, 1997.

Bebb, P. *Shopping in Regency York*. Sessions, 1994.

Books LLC. *Confectionery Companies of the United Kingdom*. Books LLC, 2010.

Bradley, J. *Cadbury's Purple Reign*. John Wiley, 2008.

Brannan, J. and F. *A Postcard from Bournville*. Bournville Trust, 1992.

Brenner, J. *The Chocolate Wars: Inside the Secret Worlds of Mars and Hershey*. Harper Collins, 1999.

Broomfield, M. *A Bournville Assortment*. Sessions, 1998.

Buijsse, B., et al. 'Chocolate consumption in relation to blood pressure and risk of cardiovascular disease in German adults'. *European Heart Journal*, 2010.

Cadbury, D. *Chocolate Wars: From Cadbury to Kraft*. Harper Collins, 2010.

Cadbury Eros Ltd. *The Bournville Story*. Cadbury's.

Chinn, C. *The Cadbury Story*. Brewin Books, 1998.

Chrystal, P. *Villages around York through Time*. Amberley, 2010.

Chrystal, P. *York Then and Now*. The History Press, 2010.

Chrystal, P. *The Confectionery Industry in York*. Pen & Sword, 2011.

Coady, C. *The Chocolate Companion*. Simon & Schuster, 1995.

Coe, S. D. *The True History of Chocolate*. Thames & Hudson, 1996.

Dickinson, J. *York on Old Postcards*. Reflections of a Bygone Age, 1989.

Dickinson, J. *50 Years of Collecting Rowntrees 1960–2010*; privately published, 2010.

Feuz, P. *Toblerone: 100 Years – The Story of a Swiss World Success*. Toblerone, 2008.

Fitzgerald, R. *Rowntree and the Marketing Revolution 1862–1969*. Cambridge University Press, 1995.

Fuller, L.K. *Chocolate Fads, Folklore and Fantasies*. Haworth Press, 1994.

Gumbley, E. *Bournville*. Market Drayton, 1991.

Harrison, M. *Bournville: Model Village to Garden Suburb*. Phillimore, 1999.

Head, B. *The Food of the Gods*. Dodo Press, 1903.

Heer, J. *Nestlé 125 Years*. Nestlé, 1991.

Hitches, M. *Bournville Steam and Chocolate*. Irwell Press, 1992.

Mayhew, H. *London Labour and the London Poor*. Oxford University Press, 1851.

Miller, M. *English Garden Cities – An Introduction*. National Heritage, 2010.

Morton, M. and F. *Chocolate – An Illustrated History*. Crown Publishers, 1986.

Moss, S. *Chocolate – A Global History*. Reaktion Books, 2009.

Needler, R. *Needlers of Hull*. Hutton Press, 1993.

Nuttgens, P. (editor). *The History of York*. Blackthorn Press, 2001.

Opie, R. *Sweet Memories*. Anova Books, 2008.

Richardson, P. *Indulgence*. Abacus, 2003.

Richardson, T. *Sweets: A History of Temptation*. Bantam Press, 2002.

Rogers, T. *A Century of Progress 1831–1931*. Cadbury's, 1931.

Rubinstein, H. *The Chocolate Book*. Penguin, 1982.

Ryan, O. *Chocolate Nations – Living and Dying for Cocoa in West Africa*. Zed Books, 2011.

Vansittart, J. *Katherine Fry's Book*. Hodder, 1966.

Vernon, A. *A Quaker Businessman – The Life of Joseph Rowntree 1836–1925*. Sessions, 1987.

Wilson, V. *The Story of Terry's*. York Oral History Society, 2009.

Windsor, D. *The Quaker Enterprise: Friends in Business*. Frederick Muller, 1980.

PLACES TO VISIT

Cadbury World, Linden Road, Bournville, Birmingham B30 2LU.
Telephone: 0121 451 4180. Website: www.cadburyworld.co.uk

Caleys Cocoa Café, The Guildhall, Gaol Hill, Norwich, Norfolk NR2 1JP.
Website: www.caleys.com/about-cocoacafe

Museum of Brands, Packaging and Advertising, 2 Colville Mews, Lonsdale Road, Notting Hill, London W11 2AR. Email:
info@museumofbrands.com. Website: www.museumofbrands.com

Thomas Tunnock Ltd, 34 Old Mill Road, Uddingston, Glasgow G71 7HH.
Telephone: 01698 813551.

La crème de la crème of the global confectionery industry as depicted in Confectionery News, *February 1938.*

INDEX